D1217778

SAFE HOUSE

Safe House

The Compelling Memoirs of the Only CIA Spy to Seek Asylum in Russia

Edward Lee Howard

An Enigma Book

Edited by Richard Coté

National Press

BOOKS

Library of Congress Cataloging-in-Publication Data

Howard, Edward Lee, 1951-
Safe House: the compelling story of the
only CIA operative to seek asylum in Russia
Edward Lee Howard
296 p. 15 x 23 cm
Includes index.
ISBN 1-882605-15-2: $23.95
1. Howard, Edward Lee
2. Defectors—United States—Biography
3. Defectors—Russia (Federation)—Biography
4. United States Central Intelligence Agency—
Officials and Employees—Biography
5. Intelligence Officers—United States—Biography
6. United States Central Intelligence Agency
7. Soviet Union. Komitet gosudarstvennoî bezopasnosti
I. Title.
JK468.I6H69   1995
327.12'092—dc20
                                        95-757
                                        CIP

PRINTED IN THE UNITED STATES OF AMERICA

10   9   8   7   6   5   4   3   2   1

Dedication

*To my family—for their help and love
throughout the past ten years.*

Contents

Publisher's Note

For many years the CIA has blamed Edward Lee Howard for the deaths of ten agents, painting him as a notorious traitor who single-handedly sacrificed the Agency's Moscow operations. One by one the damage allegedly caused by Mr. Howard has proven to have a different source: Aldrich Ames. Evidence points to the distinct possibility that the KGB fed Howard to the CIA to divert attention from their real agent, Ames. While the government spent millions to follow Ed Howard, Ames routinely drove into CIA's Langley headquarters in his new $50,000 Jaguar sedan. No red lights went off on the CIA's radar screen when Ames spent wildly, including the purchase of a half-million dollar house with cash. All on a modest government salary.

Ed Howard's story demonstrates many weaknesses in the CIA and the FBI and makes a compelling argument that he is innocent of the most serious accusations leveled against him. It is very possible that the Agency turned Howard into a spy, but the reader will have to draw his or her own conclusion.

Now that the Cold War is over, the activities of the CIA and the FBI are coming under intense scrutiny. *Safe House* sheds a bright light on many of the shortcomings of our "intelligence" operations. For someone suspected of espionage and treason to escape a dragnet of sixty FBI agents, and then some months later, to surreptitiously re-enter the United States, is not only thrilling, but frightening.

Acting as Edward Lee Howard's attorney, I submitted his manuscript to the CIA's Publications Review Board for approval. Mr. Howard, as a former CIA employee, is required to do this. The agency determined that Ed Howard has an "ongoing association with a foreign intelligence service [which] makes it inappropriate for this Agency to affirm or authenticate . . . matters that are sensitive." The CIA advised me that Mr. Howard "is not authorized to proceed with publication." To make it clear that the ban against Howard's publication applied to the publisher, the CIA threatened criminal prosecution if we proceeded without its approval.

The CIA acted as an absolute censor setting up a confrontation—we could publish the book and prepare for a legal battle with the federal government, or we could make one last ditch effort to work out an agreement.

The Justice Department expressed an interest in negotiating an out of court settlement. The ACLU agreed to join me at a Justice Department meeting which included a CIA attorney. Kate Martin, director of the ACLU's National Security Project, proved effective in convincing the Agency and the Justice Department that the First Amendment protected Mr. Howard's right of free speech and the right of the American people to read his book.

In the appendix at the back of this book are copies of letters to and from the CIA. Without the assistance of the ACLU and the Justice Department it is unlikely that you would be reading this book.

I believe that Ed Howard's story was well-worth the effort of circumnavigating the CIA censors. The only details deleted from the original manuscript are names of agents and a description of Howard's mission in Moscow. His story is a moving personal one, of choices between options far more threatening than most of us have ever faced, and he freely admits that some of those choices were wrong. Many readers, especially those in the intelligence community, may, after reading this book, think to themselves—"There, but for the grace of God, go I."

Joel D. Joseph
Publisher

Preface

Here in Moscow, I'm a Russian citizen known as Edward Janovitch. I have a good job as manager of a local business consulting firm, a spacious apartment in Moscow, a lovely dacha outside the city, and I drive a Volvo. But I'm not a run-of-the-mill, Soviet *apparatchik*. Sensitive trip wires and infra-red light beams guard my state-owned country home where armed KGB security officers protect me day and night.

Back in the United States, where I was born, my mom and dad, wife and son know me as Ed Howard, their son, husband and father. To them, I was a bright, serious young man who was born in New Mexico, went to college, married his first true love, joined the Peace Corps and ultimately went to work for the Central Intelligence Agency as an operations officer.

The CIA trained me in every aspect of clandestine spy operations in preparation for assignment to its most coveted and sensitive post: deep-cover operations from within the U.S. embassy in Moscow. I was thrilled and excited. Then, in 1983, just days before leaving for my assignment, the CIA misinterpreted a routine polygraph test, fired me and threw me out on the street.

In 1985 I fled the United States and in 1986, I defected to the Soviet Union. I've been living in exile ever since.

The U.S. government says that I am a spy who sold the KGB every secret the CIA ever taught me. They say that this came close to totally destroying the CIA's ability to spy on the Russians, and that several Russian spies were killed after I identified them. That's their side of the story. Now I am ready to tell mine.

Moscow
May 23, 1994
Edward Lee Howard

Chapter One

Just Another Air Force Brat

The Soviet government newspaper, *Izvestia*, announced that I had been granted political asylum in the Soviet Union by decree of the Supreme Soviet. A day later, the Western press exploded with news about me. I was labeled a spy and a traitor. I shuddered at how this was affecting my family, still in the United States. Deep in the heart of Mother Russia, I was protected, but my family had to withstand interrogation by the FBI and the cold, unblinking eyes of the news cameras.

My mind filled with questions. Why was I in the Soviet Union? How had I—a patriotic man whose loyalty to America had always been above reproach—become the mortal enemy of my country almost overnight?

As a child, all I ever wanted was to enjoy the outdoor life and be a cowboy on a ranch. Instead, here I was, an ex-CIA officer, living in Moscow, despised and hunted by my own government. "If only I had followed my childhood instincts and stuck to ranching," I thought! I don't believe in blaming everything bad in life on fate. Every choice I have made in my life has been with the best intentions, based on the best information available at the time. I take full responsibility for everything, good and bad, that happened as a result of those decisions.

My life got off to a good start with the great parents I inherited, but I think I got a better bargain than they. When my father, Kenneth, met and married my mother, Mary

Jaramillo, in 1950, he was a non-commissioned officer and guided missile electronics specialist stationed at Holloman Air Force Base, New Mexico. She came from a respected Hispanic-American family with deep roots in western New Mexico.

I was born in Alamogordo, New Mexico on October 27, 1951. Like my later life, Alamogordo was full of secrets; it was the town nearest the site of the first atomic bomb test in the last months of World War II.

My parents named me Edward Lee Howard, and I was baptized into the Roman Catholic church several weeks after I was born.

My father was on duty at Tachikawa Air Base in Japan when I first developed my love for ranches and the prairie. I lived with my mother on my grandparent's cattle ranch in western New Mexico, and I had a white dog named "Ricky." The ranch was small by western standards: about 2,000 acres and 100 head of cattle. My grandfather spent most of his time running the ranch, but also worked at the local sawmill to supplement his income.

Life on the ranch was simple but rewarding. I loved the colorful sunsets and the clean, dry air. For a young child, even the chores, like feeding the cattle and the chickens, were interesting. It was a simple life, but we always had enough to eat and nothing serious to complain about.

When my father returned from Japan at the completion of his two-year tour, we moved to George Air Base at Victorville, California. That started a pattern of moves known well to most military families: two years here, three years there. The frequent moves didn't bother me much, though, because all of my friends did the same. I had about as normal a childhood as anyone, with strong feelings of love for my parents and grandparents, whom I would visit in New Mexico every summer.

When I was almost five, my sister Debra was born. I started school in Denver, Colorado when I was six. I had a fairly easy time learning my lessons, but one teacher wrote that I didn't always wait to be recognized before speaking. "Whenever Ed has something to say he simply stands up and says it," said one of my grade-school report cards.

My first awareness of politics came during the 1960 presidential campaign between Richard Nixon and John F. Kennedy. I was living on an air base near Detroit, and I was able to see both of their motorcades when they came to campaign. I could feel Kennedy's charisma even though he did not shake hands with the crowd, as Nixon had done. His beautiful wife, Jackie, made quite an impression on my young mind.

In school, my class held a mock presidential debate, and I remember my teacher telling me that Kennedy would never be elected because he was a Catholic. Despite my active campaigning for Kennedy, most of my class voted for Nixon.

As a young man, I understood about as much about the Soviet Union as my contemporaries—which is to say, very little, and most of that was distorted by Cold War political perceptions. In the 1970s, most of what most Americans knew of the Soviets was based on Stalin-era stereotypes. I thought of the Soviet Union as a harsh, totalitarian state where people were forced to attend communist political education classes. The people themselves, I thought, were plump and peasant-like and all of them drank vodka every day. The land was like the North Pole and I could not imagine the sun shining anywhere there for very long. As a good, Catholic boy, I thought that the lack of sunshine was God's punishment for not allowing religion to be practiced there.

Late in 1962, with the Cold War heating up, my father was sent to Hahn Air Base, in West Germany's Hunsrck mountains, for three years. At first we lived in Kirchberg, a small village near a Mace missile site, and I would gaze at these intermediate-range missiles on their launchers every morning on my way to school. Normally, most were usually kept in the stand down (unarmed) position, but late in 1962, when the United States and the Soviet Union were eyeball-to-eyeball over Cuba, all of the missiles were raised, locked on target and ready to fire for several days.

My first overseas experience was a mixed success for me. People think that when an American military family is sent abroad, they all learn the language and get to know local people. In fact, this rarely happens, because most Americans seldom leave the base and meet only those local people who work on the base. Fortunately for me, I was required to study German at the base school and I came home with a knowledge of German, a basic understanding of Germans and Germany and a growing desire to learn more about the world.

By the time I became a teenager, I absorbed the middle-class values of my parents and the moral teachings of the Roman Catholic church. My father was a patriotic and conservative man who preached law and order, but who also believed that government should stay out of peoples' lives.

I joined the Boy Scouts of America as a boy of eight and stayed until I was sixteen. During our weekly meetings we discussed patriotic duties and we were encouraged to demonstrate our responsibilities as citizens of a free country. I participated in community projects, studied the functions of government, and proudly earned my citizenship merit badge. I also enjoyed camping out in forests for days at a time. Scouting helped my physical and moral development, and I am glad that my son, Lee, has become a Boy Scout and will enjoy these same activities.

As a boy I was also involved with the Catholic Church. I regularly attended Sunday school and served as an altar boy for two years. I enjoyed my close association with the church and even gave some thought to the priesthood. The church provided me with serenity and companionship. I never came to accept all the biblical stories, but I always respected the church and felt that its goals were admirable.

By the time I reached fifteen my interest in religion waned due to peer pressure. At the time I started college, my personal philosophy was still unshaped. I had inherited the values given me by my parents, the military community and the church, but I felt uncomfortable with many of them, especially in the area of politics.

I was also developing a growing distaste for the military establishment. I concluded that most of the military power structure was designed to protect career officers and their ultra-conservative views. By that time, I was fourteen and I wanted to travel the world, not as a military brat, but as a private citizen who could mingle with the host-country nationals. In high school, I studied Spanish and day-dreamed about traveling abroad as a scientist or a scholar.

When I was sixteen, my father was given his final overseas assignment, at Bentwaters Royal Air Force Base. From Monday through Friday, I attended Lakenheath American High School, a boarding school near Brandon, England. That was my first time away from my family, and although I missed them, I thought the boarding school experience was a great adventure.

I developed many good relationships with the American and British students I met during my year and a half at Lakenheath High. The Vietnam War and the assassinations of Robert Kennedy and Martin Luther King, Jr. took place during this tumultuous period.

At the same time, the American counter-culture was developing. People, especially young people, were standing up and questioning government policy. Why were we in Vietnam? Why not let Blacks have total equality? Why not let us smoke marijuana instead of killing our livers with alcohol? These were all powerful issues for me and my generation. Our heroes were not the government officials who rode through Washington in their black limousines. They were people like Joan Baez, who demonstrated by singing songs, or Ralph Nader, the corporate dragonslayer.

I did well in high school and graduated eighth in my class of 120 students in June 1969. I worked that summer to save money for college, and enrolled in the University of Texas at Austin the following September.

For the first time, I was on my own—almost five thousand miles away from home. I felt as most do when they leave home for the first time: apprehensive, but excited.

If my final year of high school in England had been an eye-opener, my first year at the University of Texas university was a bombshell. Coming from a high school class of 120, I found myself one of forty thousand students, lost in the sea of faces. My calculus class had as many students as my entire graduating class at Lakenheath.

Between lectures on campus, a whole new culture evolved before my eyes. Protests were held for everything from the Vietnam War to replacing the school mascot. Male students wore long hair, girls didn't wear bras, and drugs were readily available to anyone who wanted them.

I chose international business and economics as my major because I wanted to travel abroad in some professional status after graduation. The curriculum was not strenuous, and consisted largely of traditional business, economics and language courses.

The friendships I made my freshman year endured throughout my stay at the university—mainly native Texans and Hispanic-Americans who came from small, rural towns. We did all of the usual things: drank beer, played poker, went to football games and smoked a little marijuana.

The most memorable event of that era occurred at Kent State University, when the Ohio National Guard killed four students who were protesting the Vietnam War. We at the University of Texas boycotted classes, held demonstrations and confronted the state police. I was maced by state troopers when they broke up a rally we held in a campus hall. That night we gathered and passed wine bottles amongst ourselves, singing protest songs and savoring the sweet smell of marijuana. As Dickens wrote, "It was the best of times and it was the worst of times."

University was an important transitional period for me, during which I evolved away from total dependence on my family and developed a capacity for independent thinking.

I was especially fond of the writings of two political philosophers: John Locke and Thomas Jefferson. Locke's writings about individual rights paralleled my own beliefs, and I admired Jefferson for his accomplishments in the fields of agriculture, architecture, science and diplomacy.

The brilliant professor who taught National Security Politics was a former advisor to President Lyndon Johnson. Once, when he lectured on the evolution of U.S. involvement in Vietnam, liberal and conservative students clashed, exchanging shouts. The conservatives pushed the "domino theory," which predicted that leaving Vietnam would lead to the fall of Asia. The liberals wanted peace now and to let the Vietnamese choose their own political systems. My old conservative values slowly shifted to a more liberal attitude about the war and American foreign policy.

I gravitated naturally towards the international courses at university—international economics, national security politics and German. I even took a room at the German house, which was available for those who wanted to practice the language on a daily basis. I knew only that one day I wanted to work abroad, maybe for the State Department, a college or a multinational corporation.

I graduated with honors from the University of Texas in May 1972, one year ahead of schedule. I had acquired a healthy distrust for the military-industrial complex, on whom I blamed Vietnam. Like my father, I also opposed excessive government regulation of private, personal and business matters. I was in favor of President Nixon's détente with the Soviet Union because I believed that the Cold War was pointless and that cooperation was needed on global matters such as nuclear proliferation, the Middle East and the environment.

When I started my professional life, I was an independent-minded person. Perhaps it originated from the cowboy spirit I inherited from my grandparents and learned during my childhood days on the ranch, far from hospitals, fire departments and the police.

I spent the summer of 1972 working as a management trainee for Exxon Corporation in Dublin, Ireland, involved in accounting reports, sales projections and marketing meetings. The experience reinforced my taste for doing business in a foreign country. In addition, I had Dublin and the rest of Ireland to explore after my work day ended. The work was uninspiring, but the country and its people fascinating. I was intrigued by the confrontation between the Irish Republican Army and the British government. I had heard the British side of the story during my high school days at

Lakenheath High, but in Dublin I found that, as usual, there are two sides to a story.

Exxon offered me a permanent position, but I chose to enter graduate school. My future, as I saw it, was in the international arena where I already had an edge from my experience living overseas. I also wanted adventure in my life, and I wanted to be independent and never again be confined by the rigid, conservative attitudes I experienced as a military dependent. My future seemed uncertain, but promising.

A surprise awaited me on my return to university: A cable came from the U.S. Peace Corps, asking if I wanted to take a two-year assignment in Latin America as a small business advisor.

I agonized over the decision for a week. Then I opted for the real-life practical experience offered by the Peace Corps. And Latin America! The adventure I sought was around the next corner.

Chapter Two

New Horizons

I was twenty-one years old, single, idealistic and looking for adventure when I joined the Peace Corps in 1972. I was sent to Puerto Rico to join a group of small business advisors and co-op specialists. From there, to Costa Rica for three months of Spanish language training and lessons on Latin American business and agriculture. In Costa Rica, we stayed with local families. So if I wanted to eat with them, I had to learn to say in Spanish, "pass the rice," or "pass the beans."

I met Marta, a beautiful Costa Rican girl with big, brown eyes and long, dark hair. Marta was a great incentive to learn Spanish, and my Peace Corps teachers were amazed how fast I picked up the language.

My work in Colombia gave me my first exposure to poverty, disease, and primitive conditions. I still can remember eight- and nine-year old, starving children sleeping in the streets of Bogota. I visited hospitals where the sanitary conditions were no better than American bus terminals. And I remember small shoe factories where most everything was done by hand and even the accounting procedures were archaic.

I quickly fell in love with the Colombian people. They were a happy group who faced their problems with a smile and tried to enjoy each day in full. I made many Colombian friends and learned to speak Spanish fluently. At the end of my working day, I'd spend hours at the sidewalk cafes with my Colombian friends and American volunteers, discussing business problems, admiring the women and drinking beer.

My first year in Colombia was spent in Bucaramanga, and the second in Cali. The Peace Corps was the greatest two years of my life. Each day was an adventure. I worked hard Monday through Friday, and at night I'd go dancing with Columbian women.

Many of the other Peace Corps volunteers in Colombia were recreational drug users like me. On Friday and Saturday nights, we'd sometimes buy a gram or two of cocaine and share it around. In Cali, I lived in a house on a hill near Calle Sexta with two housemates: Freaky Freddie (another Peace Corps volunteer) and Alfonso. Freaky Freddie was a bearded, long-haired young man from Brooklyn who had worked on tugboats. He was a health food nut, and he'd spent most of his two-year tour in his bedroom and in the kitchen. He rarely went to work—maybe once every two weeks. His Colombian boss didn't like him, and had told him to get lost and stay lost. Freddy did as he was told.

Alfonso, a Colombian lawyer in his late 60s, was a Marxist, but he never tried to peddle his philosophies. Many of his clients were cocaine producers with legal problems. Some couldn't pay him in cash, so they paid him in cocaine. I got my cocaine from Alfonso for three dollars a gram. I wouldn't classify my drug use as drug abuse, because it never affected my behavior or the work I did. When I returned to America, I found that cocaine was $100 a gram and illegal, while wine was six dollars a bottle and legal. I made the logical choice.

Burt was another Peace Corps friend of mine in Colombia. He was a marine biologist. But when he arrived for work at the Department of Marine Biology in Buenaventura, no one had heard of him. So Burt served as a volunteer fireman during the day and as a bartender at night.

Professionally, I was getting exposure to doing business in Colombia. The firms I worked with had less than one hundred employees, most of whom were severely under-paid by any standard. Few of the firms had any medium or long-term business plans and they operated on a month-to-month basis.

I tried to develop business plans for them but my Colombian counterparts rarely took my suggestions seriously. I was naive about the extent of corruption in the Colombian government and the amount of routine bribery required for businesses to operate, and my plans failed to take this into account.

I was sent to Colombia to help its people with my professional skills and also to give the Colombian people an understanding of what America and Americans were about. When I left after two years, I found that their gifts of friendship and kindness to me far outweighed what little I was able to do for them. I left with a good, grass-roots understanding of Spanish, of Colombia, its people and culture.

The best thing to happen to me in Colombia was meeting Mary Cedarleaf, my future wife. She was also a Peace Corps volunteer when we met in Bucaramanga in the summer of 1973. We liked each other and went out a few times before I was transferred to Cali. She later said that she didn't date me more often because I had a reputation as a "fast operator" with Colombian girls. For the next three years we stayed in contact and dated a couple of times. Later, when we met in the United States in 1976, our relationship grew serious.

When I returned to the U.S.A. late in 1974, I served for a short time as a recruiter, visiting university campuses and encouraging students to enroll in the Peace Corps. I was asked to leave two campuses in Puerto Rico because the students erroneously believed that I was secretly recruiting for the CIA.

By January of 1975, I had resolved that I would work with the U. S. government in a foreign affairs capacity, but at what agency or in what position I still did not know. Washington was where the foreign service jobs were handed out, and since most agencies required graduate degrees, I enrolled at American University in Washington, D.C. to study business administration.

Culture shock is a common occurrence among Peace Corps volunteers returning home. When I returned from Colombia, I found that Americans did not understand nor care about my international experiences. Within a short time, I longed to return to Latin America where life seemed simpler, more romantic, and less materialistic than in the United States. American University was my salvation, because it enrolled many foreign students. My best friends were the Latin American and Asian students.

Just before completing my M.B.A., I was contacted by the U. S. Agency for International Development (AID) about a position with their foreign service, and I was very excited about this prospect. By this time, Mary Cedarleaf and I had reunited, fallen in love and were living together in Washington. Choosing Mary as my life partner was the best choice I have made in my life; making my biggest mistake was still a couple of years away.

After a series of in-depth interviews and an extensive background investigation, I was accepted for employment with AID and I reported to work in Washington in September, 1976. I soon learned that I would be posted to Lima, Peru. Mary and I decided to marry before I left. The ceremony was held in her family's church in St. Paul, Minnesota, on November 26, 1976. Three months later we were off to Lima.

My first year's work for AID in Lima was challenging. I was a loan officer responsible for several million dollars worth of development projects in Peru. There were two other loan officers at the mission, but I had enormous responsibility for a twenty-six year-old.

I was appalled by the living conditions for most of the Peruvian people. Rural Peruvians scratched out a living on their small farms using agricultural methods from the Middle Ages. Because they lacked any kind of reliable transportation system, they could not assure that their crops would get to market before rotting. The urban poor lived in shanty towns in dwellings made of straw mats or cardboard and they worked in cramped factories in the city.

I was fortunate in that I could speak fluent Spanish and had experience in Latin American business. Most of the AID officers and their wives did not like to travel to the Peruvian highlands or jungle, but I relished such adventure.

When I was among the Indians of the Peruvian highlands, I felt a link with my childhood days in New Mexico. I adored the altiplano as much as I did the plains of San Augustin. And, likewise, today I find myself attracted to similar parts of Siberia and especially the Lake Baikal region.

While stationed in Peru, a number of the AID and diplomatic employees purchased *huacos* (burial jars) and other pre-Colombian cultural artifacts, even though it was against the law. I was fascinated by the *huacos*, and I ultimately brought back six of them when my tour ended.

Mary and I left Lima in March, 1979 with positive feelings about Peru and its people.

My sole experience with drugs in Peru was at my going-away party at a private residence. A car was coming to take me to the airport in a couple of hours, and one of the AID people handed me a hashish pipe. I took a couple of puffs.

Since that day—in 1979—I have never used marijuana, hashish or cocaine.

Upon my return to the United States, I spent three months searching for new employment. I mailed out over one hundred résumés and had interviews with a number of companies. I had some notion that the Central Intelligence Agency (CIA) wasn't a bureaucratic organization, so I included them on my list. I did not hear from them for over a year.

Meanwhile, in June 1979 I started work in Chicago with James H. Lowry and Associates, a management consulting firm. The work was hectic but challenging. There were no bureaucratic problems, but when I found myself working on Sunday nights in preparation for Monday presentations, I looked back fondly at my old AID job. I earned a good salary and was put in charge of a small development project in Chile, which gave me the opportunity to return to Latin America twice in 1979.

In 1980 I contracted with Ecology and Environment, another consulting firm, which had a $70 million contract with the federal Environmental Protection Agency to identify and survey suspected toxic waste sites. Although I knew little about ecology or waste management, I was told not to worry. I was hired to run their regional office in Chicago, and I had access to a staff of professionals who could advise me in scientific and technical areas. My job was to keep the company operating on a profitable basis.

This new job was interesting, but not much of a challenge. The scientists took great care to brief me on their investigations concerning hazardous waste dumps and what could be done to clean them up. But I found the scientists to be childish over non-technical matters. I admired their technical skills but not their intra-office politics and petty bickering. That's when I understood why the company's senior management wanted a financial professional to control its money flow. Nevertheless, I felt quite happy in this new position and looked forward to several interesting years in Chicago. I hoped that within five years the company would go international and I could return abroad.

Mary and I bought a home just outside of Chicago and she found a good job as a recreational therapist near our home. We settled into a routine like most married couples, centered around our jobs, our home and our new friends in Chicago.

I had been with Ecology and Environment for about six months when I received my first communication from the CIA. It was appropriately mysterious, consisting of a letter on plain paper with no return address. It stated that they had received my résumé and were interested in talking with me. The letter gave a Washington, D.C. phone number which I could call collect, and it was signed by a man named Woodward.

I was curious enough to call the CIA's telephone number. I spoke with a young woman, who told me that two Agency men would soon be in Chicago and that they wanted to interview me. We agreed on an interview date.

I met the two CIA representatives in a Chicago hotel room in June of 1980. The first was a slender man from the CIA's Office of Personnel, and the second was a former operations officer named Bernie. The personnel man was cheerful and talkative. He explained the benefits and the salary levels, and apologized that I would have to take a pay cut of about $10,000 per year if I joined the CIA. Bernie, on the other hand, was somber and pessimistic. He played with his pocket knife during the entire interview.

The two men peppered me questions about my background and international experiences. The personnel man seemed to be interested in my managerial experiences, while Bernie kept asking about my personal relationships while I was overseas. When the meeting concluded, they conferred

in a separate room, then returned with an enormous application package for me to complete and mail to Washington.
I thanked them for their time, took the package, and promised to think over what they had said and mail the application package if I chose to pursue the job.

For almost two weeks, Mary and I discussed moving to
Washington and my future career possibilities at the CIA.
Although we were both content in our positions in Chicago,
we both loved the international arena. I was more eager to
take the plunge than she, but Mary agreed to support me in
whatever decision I made. I completed the application for
submission to the CIA, intending to make a final decision if
they offered me a position. My choice in accepting a position
ultimately brought about the greatest tragedy and misery
our family would ever experience.

Chapter Three

The CIA: Not Just a Bad Career Move

With my CIA application posted in June of 1980, I continued on as a regional manager for Ecology and Environment. Several months later, I began hearing from friends, neighbors and former employers that federal investigators were asking questions about me. CIA security agents even visited Horse Springs, New Mexico, where I had lived briefly as a two-year-old.

The somber investigators asked about my political attitudes, relationships with women, drinking habits, use of drugs and finances. When asked, I told my friends that the company I worked for was bidding on a government contract. The investigators' questions made my friends curious. I just told them that my company was bidding on a big government contract.

By September I was anxious to hear about the status of my application so I telephoned Washington. I was told that things were looking good and that I'd probably be invited for interviews. A month passed before I was invited to Washington for a week of medical tests, psychological examinations, a polygraph test about my personal history and lifestyle (including use of drugs, alcohol and any immoral habits), attitudinal tests, language tests and interviews with CIA officials from both the personnel and operations divisions.

The process was interesting to me, with questions like whether I preferred taking baths or showers, liked blondes or brunettes, whether I closed the bathroom door when I was home alone, or under which circumstances I would tell a lie.

Later I learned that the CIA screening process was developed to identify people who were basically honest but believed that "the ends justify the means."

It has been said that by 1980, when I was hired by the CIA, the Agency was being forced to hire less-qualified applicants than they would have preferred. The reasons given were that the American counterculture of the 1970s had made the CIA unpopular, that the Vietnam War had made military and CIA officer recruiting difficult; that terrorism was rising and that the CIA was unable to offer competitive salaries. After my defection to the Soviet Union in 1985, allegations were made that I had been some kind of substandard, marginally-qualified applicant. I'd like to address that shot now. Did the CIA settle for a second- or third-rate man when they hired me? No. If you had read my CIA employment application in 1980, you would have gotten the picture of a nearly-ideal CIA intelligence officer candidate:

- ☐ I was a healthy, twenty-nine year-old, middle-class, tri-lingual professional man who spoke English and Spanish fluently and spoke German well;

- ☐ I had a bachelor's degree from the University of Texas;

- ☐ I had a master's degree in business administration from American University;

- ☐ I already had a Top Secret security clearance from my AID work;

- ☐ I had four years of professional experience in Latin America;

☐ I had lived overseas for five years in Germany and England;

☐ I had professional experience as a small business expert, AID loan officer and regional administrator at Ecology and Environment.

In all, my educational, professional and business references were top-flight. At the time I joined the CIA, I already had a well-paid, upper-management position with Ecology and Environment. I passed the examinations, met all of their hiring criteria and I was invited to join the CIA in December, 1980. I was told to report for work at CIA headquarters in Langley, Virginia on the last day of President Carter's administration in January, 1981.

Even after I received the acceptance letter, I still wasn't sure I wanted to join the CIA. Accepting the job meant moving and selling our comfortable house, leaving a good job with a higher salary, and returning to government work from the private sector. On the positive side it meant adventure, a real chance at some interesting foreign work and being inside the world's most mysterious secret society.

"What's money?" I said to myself. "We can always buy a new house and make new friends." I thought about the CIA assignment possibilities in Europe, and reasoned that I could always leave the Agency if I didn't like it. I decided to accept the CIA's offer and become a spook.

I reported to Washington on the appointed date to join a group of twenty-five other new recruits. Mary remained in Chicago for five months to sell our home and wrap up her work.

After being sworn in by John MacMahon, the CIA Deputy Director for Operations, it was explained that our first year in the CIA would be devoted to the "career trainee" (CT) program. It was a trial period for both the new CT's and the

CIA. For the first month we would attend lectures on the organization of the U.S. intelligence community and the CIA. We would then be rotated to various desk assignments in headquarters and then sent for eighteen weeks of operational intelligence training at Camp Peary (nicknamed "The Farm") near Williamsburg, Virginia.

I remember that my first day at the CIA's Langley, Virginia headquarters was quite exhilarating. Almost everything I saw was labeled "secret." At the end of the day we had our first security lecture and were given our CIA identification badges. About thirty percent of our class was called into private conferences with security officers. I was one of them. I was told that although it had been a long time since I last used cocaine (1974) or smoked marijuana (1979), I would be fired from the CIA if I did so again.

My first feeling of uneasiness about the CIA came within two weeks of my hiring. My class was getting a lecture from the chief the CIA's Special Operations Group, and the lecturer was outlining the CIA's paramilitary operations in Central America and Africa. During the lecture I recalled a document that I was required to sign when I joined the CIA. It stated that I acknowledged knowing about and understanding the law which states that no military action may be taken in a foreign country without Congressional approval.

I raised a question with the lecturer about whether our paramilitary operations had been properly authorized, given the legal requirement for Congressional approval. His response was icy and harsh. The lecturer stared me down and stated that our operations were approved by the "highest authority"—at the White House. His response left little doubt that the CIA gave itself considerable flexibility in choosing to whom they went for permission when they wished to stir up foreign mischief. Given the attitude of the ex-military members of my class, I didn't pursue the matter, but the answer made me uneasy.

After four weeks of orientation lectures I was assigned to a desk in the CIA's European division. For me it was a new experience to be a clerk. In Chicago, I was a division manager with my own private secretary; now I had to type my own documents and do my own filing. The other CT with me on the European desk often joked that James Bond was really a GS-5! The experience taught me never again to take a secretary for granted.

The routine at Langley was much the same for the next six months. After the European desk, I rotated to the covert action desk of the International Activities division. The work was more stimulating than the previous assignment since it involved economic intelligence—and this was more in line with my professional interests. Here I gained some insight into the size of the CIA bureaucracy and its paper trails: I dealt with ream after ream of reports, studies and files. It was here I learned that most CIA employees are not spies—they are secretaries, file clerks, analysts and technicians.

The CIA's compartmentalized security system extends all the way down to its cafeterias. There are two cafeterias at Langley: one for overt (known) employees, and another for covert (undercover) employees like me. During my breaks from the desk work I met and socialized with my classmates in the covert cafeteria. We talked about our different assignments and gossiped about operations.

In August, 1980 my class was shipped off to Camp Peary for intelligence operations training. Although The Farm is officially designated a Department of Defense facility, it is well-known that Peary is the CIA's boot camp for spies and the training center for many of its special operations.

We were housed in modern quarters, two students to a room. There were dining facilities, a gymnasium, a bar, and a classroom building. Camp Peary itself is sparsely populated; it is surrounded by pine trees, lovely, small ponds and rolling hills.

For the next eighteen weeks I spent hour after hour from Sunday evening until Friday afternoon, slaving away on my intelligence exercises. The routine is long and arduous, beginning with physical training and light hand-to-hand combat. We learned the tricks of the spy trade ("tradecraft," to spooks and spy novelists), including clandestine photography, lock picking, the use of disguises, intelligence agent recruitment and management exercises. Every exercise was evaluated and graded, and the instructors made no attempt to spare their criticism. They demanded perfection.

During this intense training, I formed close relationships with three of my classmates, two men and one woman. We were older than the others and had overseas experience. We also shared a dim view of the ex-military students who, for the most part, preferred to solve problems with their muscles rather than their minds.

We were graded on a one-to-seven scale on every exercise we studied at The Farm, and at the end of the training, all the grades were added up. They released the cumulative ratings a couple of days before graduation in December 1981 and I was in the top twenty-fourth percentile.

Those who did best at The Farm got the best posts: Western and Eastern Europe; the students who did less well were assigned to Africa or Latin America. I requested and was assigned to the European division.

Most of my classmates wanted an assignment to the elite Soviet division, but I never had any interest in going to Moscow. My dream assignment was economic officer in an embassy like Berne, Switzerland, working with bankers and gathering economic intelligence.

The European division assigned me to work on the East German desk. I was intrigued by the East German assignment but my heart still longed for economic work in Switzerland. About a month after I started work at the German desk, the personnel officer for the CIA's Soviet division invited my wife and me for tea at her house in McLean, Virginia. We went and were astounded by her proposal: she wanted me to accept an assignment to Moscow.

She told me that the experience would be a major asset to my career, and that after Moscow, I could have almost any assignment I desired. Although this amounted to yet another "Plan B" career move, Mary and I discussed it for a couple of days and I decided to accept the offer, based chiefly on the premise that it would be a rung up the CIA career ladder for me. It wasn't, but the reasons weren't to become clear for some time. And by then, it would be far, far too late to do anything about it.

I was transferred to the Soviet desk in February, 1982 and began my Russian language training shortly thereafter. Although I spoke fluent Spanish and some German, I had never tried Russian and feared the experience. After all, I was over thirty, and the older you get, the harder the languages become.

The European division had been a fun place to work and the people who worked there liked to socialize both on and off the job. The Soviet division, in contrast, was a cold, sober place. There was little fun on the job and very little socializing after hours.

The managers of the Soviet division were a bitter group of people. There were some Russian emigrés who seemed straight out of the White Army Corps. They seemed to spit out the word, "Soviet," when they pronounced it and they suspected everyone and everything.

When something went wrong in Moscow it was always blamed on the *Komitet Gosudarstevennoy Bezopasnosti,* or KGB—the Soviet Committee of State Security. If one of our officers got a flat tire on his car, it was chalked up to the KGB. If someone in Moscow found some yellow dust on his car's steering wheel, no one suspected tree pollen—it was the KGB.

I was glad to leave the desk to begin my specialized training for Moscow. It included the Denied Areas Operations Course: training in how to detect surveillance and escape if detected. Mary participated in this training with me, as she would be a valuable resource for me in Moscow. The training was so long and demanding that we had no time to care for our pet dog, and we had to give her away. Once we completed the special course for operations in the USSR, I was considered to be in the "pipeline." This meant that I had completed all requirements for the assignment and had been accepted for work at the Soviet desk.

Next I started Russian language training at Georgetown University in Washington. In the fall of 1982 I continued my Russian studies at the CIA Language Institute at Arlington, Virginia. Russian was a difficult language for me to learn, and even today, if I leave Russia for any extended period of time, it quickly slips away.

By January of 1983 I was finished with most of my language training and was assigned for training at the U.S. State Department in preparation for my assignment to Moscow the following June.

After my defection, much was made about the CIA's logic (or lack of it) in choosing Ed Howard, a highly-trained but unproven intelligence officer, for this sensitive, ultra-high priority assignment. While it pains me to give the CIA credit for showing good judgment, their choice to send me to Moscow, like their choice to hire me in the first place, was perfectly logical and completely understandable. Just put yourself in their place:

For this sensitive job, the CIA wanted somebody that the KGB would never suspect. They were looking for someone who had a squeaky-clean résumé, and they put themselves in the shoes of the KGB: who would you least suspect? Answer: Ed Howard, the idealistic, former Peace Corps volunteer. That was one of my strengths.

They also wanted someone who was mature. The average age in my CIA recruit class was about twenty-five; I was thirty by the time I was picked for assignment to Moscow. I also had the international experience, and had graduated in the top quarter of my class at The Farm.

Some have said that since I was a former drug user with some drinking problems, the CIA should never have given me the sensitive, Moscow assignment. Here's how the CIA looked at it: my former drug use was no more serious or unusual than that of the other thirty percent of my CT classmates who were also former drug users. And although the CIA and FBI deny it, occasional—or even sustained—alcohol abuse is just as common among their officers is as it is among many other professionals in high-pressure lines of work.

The bottom line was this: my training results were outstanding, my background was perfect, and my former drug use and current alcohol problems were not unusual. That's why I was picked to become a deep-cover intelligence officer at the U.S. embassy in Moscow.

My cover for these clandestine technical operations was to be a second secretary of the embassy. For that, the Agency sent me to foreign service officer training classes at the State Department. I enjoyed my time at the State Department, and I made good friends there. My State Department colleagues were a good-natured bunch both on and off the job. None of them knew I was really a CIA officer, and I preferred it that way. I found them to be as hard-working and intelligent as my CIA colleagues, but much more progressive and liberal in their thinking.

I soon came to dread visiting the Soviet desk at Langley, and I only went there once or twice a week when I had to. Perhaps it was the quasi-military mentality of my CIA colleagues that distorted my feelings about Langley, but I found myself thinking of transferring to the State Department for work as an economic specialist as soon as my two years in Moscow were over. Even my wife noticed the difference in the two groups, and I know that she, too, felt more at home with the State Department people than with our CIA colleagues.

Our son, Lee, was born in March of 1983. It was a big event for us, as it is for any first-time parents. All of a sudden, many big things were happening all at once in my life. I was preparing to go to Moscow. I was leading an uneasy double life with my State Department and normal friends in Washington, and now we had a new member of the family.

I privately wondered what else could happen and only hoped that things would go well for me in Moscow. I was aware of the dangers of my assignment and had heard many horror stories about the KGB and their harassment of U.S. diplomats. Little did I know then that I had little to fear from the KGB. The worst problems of my life were to come from my own kind—and soon.

Chapter Four

Those Wiggly Lines

I was fired by the CIA just before I was scheduled to depart for my deep cover assignment at the U.S. embassy in Moscow. My employment was terminated solely on the basis of a series of four conflicting polygraph tests administered at Langley in March of 1983. The CIA just told me to resign. It was a great shock. To this date, they have never given me a reason for my dismissal.

Because no machine can unerringly recognize when a person is lying, and because its results are unpredictable and inconclusive, polygraph results are not admissible as legal evidence in the United States and many foreign countries. But don't try to tell this to the CIA, which attributes almost mystical powers to the polygraph. To give you an idea of what went on, let me tell you about the polygraph and how the CIA used it on me.

The polygraph test is based on the theory that there are physical reactions to lying which can be consistently identified and accurately measured.

The machine itself is a recording device which measures certain physical responses to being questioned: breathing rate, blood pressure and sweating. The subject is seated, and a pneumograph tube is fastened around his chest to measure his respiration rate. An ordinary blood pressure cuff measures pressure and pulse, and electrodes attached to the fingers measure increased sweat-gland activity, which reduces the skin's ability to carry electrical current. The output of these sensors is recorded in the form of wavy ink lines on a strip of moving paper. An interrogator asks a series of yes/no questions, and the polygraph record is later evaluated by one or more interpreters.

According to several polygraph experts I have spoken with since my firing, many factors can affect the accuracy of a polygraph test. If it records emotional stress, for example, that stress could be the result of lying—or of a fight with a loved one, a recent fender-bender or financial problems. Pathological liars, on the other hand, show almost no bodily response when telling lies, the experts say. Ordinary nervousness, physical or mental abnormalities, discomfort, excessive pretest interrogation or even indifference to a question can all affect the accuracy of a polygraph test. To top it off, the "lie detector," as it is often referred to, can fail to detect lies seventy-five percent of the time if the subject takes a mild tranquilizer before testing.

The testing procedure itself has to be very carefully conducted in order not to influence the results. The room used for the test should be plain, quiet, comfortable and private. The examiner's role is also important. He should be unemotional, consistently objective and thoroughly trained in scientific interrogation to reduce the chance for human error.

The CIA routinely uses polygraphs to screen its employees for security risks. New employees are tested before they are hired, before they embark on major assignments, and at routine, five-year intervals. When I took my pre-employment polygraph, I told the CIA all about my use of cocaine and marijuana in South America, my occasional overuse of alcohol and some minor, boyhood thefts. I met all of their hiring criteria, passed their polygraph test, and was hired.

All CIA officers are tested before they leave for service in a socialist country and immediately upon their return. In April of 1983 I knew I was going to Moscow and also knew that I was due for a routine polygraph test. Oddly enough, no one had said anything to me about the test, and I was all set for Moscow. I knew the policy, so I called the security section and said, "Shouldn't I have a polygraph?"

They said, "Yes." That was my mistake. If I hadn't said anything, I probably wouldn't be in the position I'm in today. I took the test and thought it went just fine, because the polygraph operator, a pleasant man in his late twenties, smiled, shook my hand and wished me a good trip to Moscow. But two days later my office phone rang, and someone from the security section said that they'd like me to take another polygraph.

I said okay, walked downstairs, and was greeted by an older man. He said that some of the indications of the first test didn't look quite right to the interpreters. There were some signs of deception about crime, he said. I took the second test, and the operator, who was thoughtful and considerate, said, "There's still some problem areas here. There's something about crime you're hiding. Go home and write down every crime or theft you've ever committed."

When I joined the CIA I was required to list every item I had ever stolen (like the time I was nine and stole some carrot seeds) and every law I had ever broken, no matter how trivial (like drinking a couple of beers while driving home). I completed the list and returned it to them. I couldn't see what on earth they were getting upset about, as I had been totally honest about each and every misdeed in my past, including my drug use in South America and my occasional abuse of alcohol.

For thirty months, the CIA had been training me to commit crimes against the Soviet Union, including techniques to carry on surreptitious break-ins and steal information. When they asked me about crimes, it's possible that I had some subconscious feelings which the polygraph brought to the surface. I'll never know.

In any case, things continued to deteriorate, and I was called in to take a third test. By this time, I was getting nervous about the call-backs, and I asked my mother-in-law, a physician, to prescribe me a mild tranquilizer. I took one of the pills just before taking the third test. This one was administered by a real, hard-ass son-of-a-bitch they called, "The Hammer."

In a military "command voice," he told me: "Sit down. Face front. Don't look at me. Don't look to the side." He sounded and acted like a drill instructor, and he tried to intimidate me. When he asked me if I had taken drugs that day, I answered "yes," and told him about the prescribed tranquilizer. He hit the roof, because he knew (although I didn't at the time) that taking a mild tranquilizer can usually enable a person who lies to beat the polygraph.

The Hammer questioned me again and again about drug use and drinking, and on Friday, April 29, 1993, he gave me yet another polygraph test—my fourth. Apparently he was pleased with this last one, and he thanked me for coming, smiled, and shook my hand as I left.

I was so relieved that this testing ordeal was over that I went to a grocery store in nearby McLean, Virginia, bought some snacks and a bottle of good champagne and went home to celebrate with Mary and my in-laws, who were visiting us at the time. We all relaxed, had a good time, and celebrated our imminent move to Moscow.

On Monday afternoon, May 2, 1983, I got a call to report to the CIA personnel office. I walked in the door and asked, "What's up?" They demanded that I resign on the spot or they would fire me. They refused to tell me why I was being fired, and they didn't say anything about drugs or alcohol. They never talked to my supervisors to see if I was having any problems at work (I wasn't). They simply informed me that the Agency wanted my resignation, and that there was no avenue of appeal.

The Agency didn't offer me another, less-sensitive assignment, or any kind of probation. They didn't tell me what I did wrong, nor offer me any way to clear my good name. They didn't even offer me the two weeks' notice you'd give a bag boy at a supermarket. I was dismissed, effective immediately.

Security officers escorted me to a secretary's desk, and I saw that she was already typing up my résumé. Ex-CIA officers are not permitted to list the CIA as an employment reference, so she asked me what I wanted to have listed as my most recent position. "Economic specialist with the State Department," I said, numbly.

That was it. I wasn't going to Moscow. I wasn't going anywhere—except out the door. End of career. I had been driving a CIA car, and they asked me for the keys at once, then and there. I had to take the bus home.

I was kept on the payroll through the end of June, when I left Washington for New Mexico. Before I left the capital, they requested that I visit the CIA staff psychiatrist, just to make sure I wasn't overly angry about being fired. Their attitude seemed to be, "We stuck the knife in your back and won't tell you why, but don't take it personally."

They also told me over and over again to come in for a physical examination, but by that time, I wanted nothing more from them. I was sick of the CIA and everything associated with it. But they kept calling the house, asking Mary to help get me in for a physical.

I made several calls to the embassy in Moscow after my firing. Foreign service officers and embassy staff frequently have to call back and forth between the embassy and the

State Department in Washington. In the United States, we had a telephone number which we could dial from anywhere in the United States and be connected directly to the U.S. embassy in Moscow. It was a conventional, "open" (unprotected) phone line used for routine, unclassified conversations, so we assumed that the KGB listened to those calls. At the Moscow end, a Marine guard answered the phone and made the connection to the proper extension in the embassy.

I had several friends at the embassy, one of whom was Jim Smith. When I told Jim that I was not coming, he told me that he had already heard about it and asked what had happened. I didn't tell him about the polygraph tests, but I shared with him that I was angry about the whole affair. "The assholes don't believe me," I said, "and I've been asked to resign."

I knew that there were suspected KGB agents at the embassy, because the CIA suspects all Soviet employees to be potential spies. If I had been in contact with the KGB before I defected—and I was not—I would never have been crazy enough to contact a KGB officer over an open telephone line through the U.S. embassy in Moscow.

The CIA had trained me to be a sophisticated spy. If I had wanted to contact the KGB, I would have done so secretly. I would have made a covert phone call to the Soviet embassy in Mexico City, or I would have called via a pay phone, but I would never make a call to the KGB via the U.S. embassy on an open line. No professional intelligence officer is that stupid.

When the CIA called yet another time to get me to take a physical examination, I said to myself, "I'll give them the message in no uncertain terms that I don't want their damn physical." I called the embassy on the special line, got the Marine guard, and asked to be connected to the CIA Chief of Station in Moscow. He was not in and I left a message: "I'm not taking my physical." He, of course, already knew that my assignment had been canceled—but now, the KGB almost certainly knew, too.

Under a reciprocal agreement, the United States government must notify the host country when each of its staff members arrives and departs. Consequently, the Soviets knew that a foreign service officer named Edward Lee Howard was due to arrive in Moscow in June, 1983 to take the position of second secretary of the embassy. My call to the CIA station chief about the physical effectively revealed to the Soviets that my job was to have been a deep-cover CIA officer. I made that call deliberately and in anger, because they kept calling me to have the physical and I wanted to get their attention. I did.

Langley quickly learned that I had made this call to the embassy. They called me at my home and said, "We have to see you, and you know why." I went in and met with the deputy chief of the Soviet division. He lectured me about this supposed telephone security violation, and I told him I had made the call to get them to stop harassing me about the physical.

That telephone call put my name at the top of the CIA's "disgruntled ex-employee" list. And the KGB, who now knew that the CIA's prospective deep-cover officer in Moscow had been fired and was resentful, probably put me on their "we-need-to-talk-to-this-guy-as-soon-as-possible" list.

The KGB had to wait over two years for that talk—but talk, we did.

Chapter Five

Ed Howard, Ex–Spy

As of May 3, 1983, I, Edward Lee Howard, CIA-trained spy, was out of a job. After what I had been through, I had no further interest in the intelligence business. Fortunately, I had an impressive work record before the CIA, and if my CIA-period references were checked by a future employer, the report would come back that Edward L. Howard, a "foreign service officer for the State Department," had resigned for personal reasons.

The week after my firing was hard on me and my wife. I was in a state of shock. I had always excelled in every previous career assignment, and my personal integrity had never been challenged. I was disoriented by the way they had pulled the rug out from under me—and angered by the callous way they had fired me and thrown me out on the street. They kept me on the payroll for several weeks and asked me to see their psychiatrist, Dr. Bernard Malloy. I visited him several times, but he seemed far more interested in limiting my potential damage to the CIA than in helping me.

At home, Mary and I had some fast decisions to make. All the plans we had made for two years in Moscow were in tatters. We had to come up with a "Plan B" for our lives. I decided to leave Washington and return to my first two loves: economics and New Mexico. In June of 1983, we rented out our Washington home until it could be sold, packed the car, and drove home to the cattle country I loved so much.

I tried to focus on the future and on the positive aspects of my situation. I was happy to return to New Mexico and to find a job I could talk about with my family and friends. That part was especially appealing to Mary. We were both disillusioned and disoriented, yet hopeful.

In April of 1983, when I had been undergoing State Department training, I had filled out an application for my diplomatic passport. At that time I was planning to visit Dallas and spend a week with my parents before traveling to Moscow. The form asked where the passport should be sent, and I put my parents' address in Dallas.

The passport was issued April 26, 1983. I was dismissed from the CIA on May 2. Nevertheless, the State Department forwarded it to the Soviet embassy, to get a multiple-entry, diplomatic visa entered onto it. That took place on May 18, 1983, some sixteen days after I was fired. Then the passport was returned to the State Department, where a clerk mailed it to me in Dallas, where it awaited me—an incredible bureaucratic blunder.

The CIA terminated me and sixteen days later took my diplomatic passport to the Soviet embassy, obtained a multiple-entry visa and mailed the passport to me. There, on page five, it declared, "Department of State, Washington. The bearer is abroad on an assignment for the foreign service of the United States of America." With that passport, the U.S. government had officially established my diplomatic credentials with the Soviets. I kept it as a souvenir.

In New Mexico, I found myself depressed, and I turned to alcohol. My drinking, which had already caused considerable friction in my marriage, increased.

My problems with alcohol snuck up on me gradually. When I was with U.S. AID in Peru, alcohol was cheap at the

U.S. embassy commissary, and I did a lot of social drinking at embassy cocktail parties.

When I came back to the United States, my drinking decreased until I joined Ecology and Environment. The senior staff did a lot of weekend drinking and entertaining, but that didn't cause any major problems for me. My serious drinking started while I was working for the CIA in 1981 and 1982. About that time, Mary began voicing her objections about my alcohol intake on weekends and after work. These problems increased after I was fired, and led to a great deal of grief the next few years.

Late in June of 1983 I answered an ad in the *Albuquerque Journal* for a position as an economic analyst with the New Mexico state government. I was interviewed by Curtis Porter, director of the Legislative Finance Committee, and Philip Baca, his deputy. They were impressed with my credentials, and they liked the fact that I was a New Mexico native. They offered me a salary of $30,000 and asked if I could start immediately.

We were able to sell our house in Virginia for about $110,000 and we moved into a one-story, adobe-style house at 108 Verano Loop, in El Dorado, a nice suburban development about twenty minutes south of Santa Fe.

I soon grew to like my supervisor, Curt Porter, and enjoyed my work. It consisted largely of analyzing and projecting income for the state of New Mexico. I got along well with the legislators, the committee chairmen and the members of the executive branch. They all seemed pleased with my work.

Mary and I settled into a typical, suburban lifestyle. We entertained a lot at home, and I sometimes drank too much at these occasions. I also developed a number of drinking buddies among the state government employees and politicians.

New Mexico derives much of its income from oil and gas taxes, and my work called for me to travel to many economic conferences, especially those concerned with oil and gas production.

One of those trips came on October 20, 1983, when I traveled to the Washington area to attend a taxation and revenue conference for the New Mexico legislative delegation being held in Williamsburg, Virginia.

While I was walking the streets of Washington during that trip, an eerie feeling came over me when I passed the Soviet consulate. I sat down on a park bench nearby and wondered to myself (as I imagine many a CIA operations officer has), "What would happen if I walked through that door and told them everything I know?"

Almost everyone has fantasies: doctors, lawyers, judges, ministers, dentists, airline pilots and secretaries. But most never act on them. That's what makes fantasies so great: you can imagine doing the unthinkable—but never have to pay the consequences for acting them out. Yes, I debated in my mind the morality of such an action, the likelihood that I would be taken seriously (or thrown out as a crank), and the possible benefits and liabilities.

But let the record be clear: at no time before September 23, 1985 did I ever walk into a Soviet embassy or consulate in Washington or anywhere else. Neither did I ever write, mail or deliver them a letter suggesting that I had anything to give or sell them. I never met the Soviets or asked anything of them until I fled the FBI, escaped from the United States, walked into the Soviet consulate in Helsinki on September 23, 1985 and asked for their protection.

The most embarrassing event of my life took place on the evening of February 26, 1984. It was an event that would haunt me for the rest of my life.

In the United States, I was a gun owner and a licensed gun dealer, although I obtained the dealer's license mostly for the savings it would bring me when I purchased a weapon. I owned a .44 Magnum revolver, and I decided to go out into the desert one night for some target shooting. I put the gun under the seat of my Jeep and headed out, but I had a few too many beers while I was at home, and I decided to stop at a restaurant. I got involved in a stupid argument with three men, and I got badly beaten. I pulled out the gun to scare them. It went off, shooting a hole through the roof of a car belonging to one of them. The police arrived soon after and arrested me for assault with a deadly weapon. I spent the night in jail.

After reviewing the case and looking at my background, the prosecutor reduced the charge to three counts of aggravated assault. I knew that alcohol had gotten me into this horrible mess, and I voluntarily contacted a New Mexico state program that provides substance abuse and psychological counseling. I stuck with this program until September of 1985.

My attorney and I worked out a plea bargain to end the case. I agreed to plead guilty to three counts of aggravated assault and to five years probation. I agreed to undergo a psychological evaluation, comply with whatever the psychologist recommended, and to compensate the man whose car I damaged. I was also prohibited from leaving New Mexico without the permission of the court, except on official business trips for the state.

On March 28, 1984, I left on a business trip to an energy conference in New Orleans, where I met an old friend of mine, Fred Johnson. Fred had also been fired by the CIA, and we had a good time that night, partying and drinking on Bourbon Street and joking about how much fun it would be to "screw the CIA." I had a good Peace Corps buddy,

Richard Marchese, in Mexico City, and we laughed about how it would blow the minds of the CIA surveillance officers who kept track of the Soviet embassy there if Fred Johnson and I went to Mexico City, saw him, and then visited the Soviet embassy! It was nothing more than two drunks bullshitting with each other. I never had any real plan to go to the Soviet embassy in Mexico City, nor did I ever get plane tickets or anything else. Much later, the CIA would interview Fred Johnson and hear about the conversation. The FBI twisted this story into an allegation that I was already a KGB spy and wanted to bring Fred Johnson in with me.

On the Fourth of July weekend of 1985 I visited Fred Johnson, who was then living at South Padre Island, Texas. Again, my sense of humor got me in trouble. I was staying at his condo. We went to a wine store and bought three bottles of fine wine. They were about fifteen dollars a bottle, not five or six dollars, like the wine I usually bought. I put them in Fred's refrigerator, and when he saw the labels, and said, "Where did you get all the money to spend on wines?"

I looked at him, smiled, and said flippantly, "I got it from my Soviet case officer."

He laughed, and I laughed, and that was it. Until I heard that it showed up in his affidavit to the FBI as a statement of fact, not a piece of typical, intelligence officer humor. If a man was going to confess to having a relationship with Soviet intelligence, he wouldn't do it in one, flippant remark as he's putting the wine bottles in the refrigerator. That idea was total nonsense, but over the next two years, the FBI was going to build a case against me with nonsense like that.

About a week after my return from the conference in Washington, I was visited by George Morgan, my former boss at the CIA's Soviet desk, and Bernard Malloy, the CIA psychiatrist. They came to see me for several reasons. A short time before, I had visited Morgan's home one evening to talk about my firing and tell him about my frustrations. They also came because I had filed a workmen's compensation claim to get money for psychological counseling after my firing. They took me to lunch and handed me an envelope containing cash, and asked me to sign under my old CIA pseudonym, Edward Houston. The cash was to pay for the psychological counseling I was required to get after the shooting incident. It was a couple hundred dollars.

I also had a lengthy conversation with them about my firing, how they screwed it up, and my resentment about the whole affair. I told them about the time I stopped outside the Soviet consulate in Washington, but I made it clear to both of them that I didn't go in or give anything to the Soviets.

During that visit, Dr. Malloy said that the CIA would pay for additional psychological counseling. Anyone treating an ex-CIA employee has to have a full background investigation and receive a security clearance by the Agency. They told me to choose a psychiatrist and contact them before I told him anything. I chose Dr. Michael Dudelczyk, in Santa Fe. It took them months to do the background check, but they finally approved him in October of 1984. I started seeing him twice a month starting just after Christmas, 1984. I talked with him about my alcohol problems, and he was pleasant, but not very helpful. I saw him at irregular intervals until September of 1985.

In 1984 and 1985 I made three trips to Europe which later came under intense FBI scrutiny. It has been alleged that I met with the KGB and passed them information during one or more of these trips. This is completely untrue, and to this day, no one has produced a single shred of hard evidence that I colluded with the Soviets before I arrived in Helsinki on September 23, 1985.

Later, when the FBI interrogated me, I told them, "If you really want to track down a businessman, get his American Express card receipts. If you think I'm hiding anything about these trips, just look at my American Express card receipts. They'll tell you where I've been." Since I have absolutely nothing to hide, I will tell you about these three trips now.

In July of 1984, Mary and I planned a week-long trip to Europe with Lee. We planned to combine pleasure with business: I was going to attend a conference on oil price forecasting in Milan which was hosted by Data Resources, Inc. (DRI). I showed my boss, Curtis Porter, the DRI conference brochure, and I told him I'd pay all my own expenses if he'd give me permission to attend. He approved, and we flew to Frankfurt, Germany on Saturday, September 15, 1984.

Mary and I have different recollections of the order that we visited different cities on this trip, but my recollection follows. We rented a car in Frankfurt on the 15th and arrived in Zurich the next day. There we stayed at the Movenpick Hotel. From there, we drove through Lucerne to Milan, where I found that the DRI conference had been canceled. We stayed there for a day, did some sightseeing and continued on with our trip.

The next morning, I called my friends Marco Ferroni and Ann Strattner. They lived in a little village named Sariswil, just outside of Berne. Marco and Ann distinctly remember that we arrived from Milan. We spent two days and nights with them, and they took us sightseeing throughout the neighboring villages. We left their house near Berne on Thursday, the 20th, and entered Austria. On the night of the 20th, we stayed in the little village of St. Anton, just over the Austrian border.

After we settled in at the inn, Mary and I had a fight. I wanted to go out; she wanted to stay in. I had a couple of drinks at the inn, and went out for a short drive. I had dinner and another drink, and I was back within an hour.

From St. Anton we turned north before we reached Innsbruck and drove on to Munich the next day to visit the Oktoberfest. We arrived there on Saturday, the 22nd of September, and then drove back to Frankfurt. We flew home on Sunday, and I went back to work on Monday.

Various allegations have been made that I contacted the KGB in Vienna on that trip. This is not true. Mary and I were together every minute of those nine days except for about an hour in St. Anton, and neither we together nor I on my own went to Vienna during this trip.

In April of 1985, Mary and I were able to acquire inexpensive airline tickets and flew to Vienna for a brief, four-day vacation. This trip was exclusively for fun. We visited our friends, Marco Ferroni and Ann Strattner, again, and also visited Zurich, where I indulged a long-time fantasy of mine and spent $600 on a Rolex watch.

In August of 1985 I made my third trip to Europe. I told my boss that my grandmother had died in Michigan, but I flew alone to Zurich on Wednesday, the 7th. I was there to sell the *huacos* I had purchased in Peru and get back quickly, because I had no official reason for being out of New Mexico, and was therefore in violation of my probation.

I scouted Zurich for a day or two, found a couple of galleries who were potential buyers, and eventually sold six *huacos* to the Merrin Gallery in Zurich for about 10,000 Swiss francs, worth about $4,500 at the time.

I returned to the United States on Monday, August 12, with the proceeds of the sale. That money would become part of the famous "$10,000 in the desert," which the FBI would suggest came from the KGB.

The most painful period in my life began on August 1, 1985, when a KGB colonel named Vitali Sergeevich Yurchenko walked into the U.S. embassy in Rome and requested political asylum. Yurchenko was one of the men in charge of the KGB's U.S. operations, and he was quickly flown to CIA headquarters at Langley, then driven to a safe house in Virginia.

I will go into more detail later about the Yurchenko affair, but now I will be brief. In the first week of August, 1985, he told his CIA and FBI debriefers that there were two moles (American agents working for the Soviets) inside the U.S. intelligence community. The first, he said, had red hair, worked in communications and lived in a suburb of Washington. That man turned out to be Ronald W. Pelton, an officer of the super-secret National Security Agency. Pelton had been selling U.S. naval communications secrets to the Soviets.

The second mole he knew only by the code name, "Robert," who was described as a disgruntled, ex-CIA employee who had been assigned to Moscow but whose assignment had been canceled. Yurchenko said that he had never met Robert.

It took the CIA debriefers only one phone call to determine who Yurchenko was talking about. They called George Morgan at the Soviet desk and he told them immediately: Robert could only be Ed Howard.

Based solely upon Yurchenko's description of "Robert," and upon no evidence whatsoever of their own, the CIA concluded that I was a Soviet spy. As I will explain later, Yurchenko was using information the KGB had gleaned about me in 1983 from routine diplomatic sources and "open" communications lines to construct a "straw man" who could be offered up to the CIA to draw fire away from their major, active mole: Aldrich Ames. My CIA work history and subsequent behavior after I was fired made me the perfect patsy.

Even though I had never been approached or recruited by the KGB, my background and history made me a perfect target for recruitment—a fact which would be obvious to both sides. Yurchenko's credibility with his debriefers was high, and he had already exposed Pelton. Given the low regard in which the CIA held me, there was no reason for them to doubt that I was a Soviet spy. Yurchenko's plan of offering me up as a false target to distract the CIA and FBI from probing deeper for the real mole was simple, elegant, and worked like a charm.

The CIA was now in a real bind. For the two years after firing me, they had been covering up the fact that they considered me a loose cannon, and they had never told the FBI about my phone calls to the U.S. embassy, sitting outside the Soviet consulate or that they were paying for my psychiatrist. Now they would have to tell them everything about me and explain why they had kept it secret from the FBI all this time.

With its characteristic lack of candor, the CIA pondered what to do for three or four days before telling the FBI that Robert's profile matched my CIA work history. At the end of Yurchenko's first week here, the CIA finally informed the FBI about me. Within days, the FBI mounted a massive investigation to determine the recent history, whereabouts and current activities of their newest "wanted" man: Edward Lee Howard, suspected traitor.

It was alleged that I was in collusion with the Soviets by August 1, 1985, when Yurchenko defected. I made my trip to Vienna to sell the *huacos* on August 7. For the purposes of discussion, let's assume that I was a paid agent of the KGB at the time of my Vienna trip, and that the purpose of that trip, as was also alleged, was to "reel me in" and give me instructions.

Put yourself in the KGB's shoes. You would have to assume that Yurchenko had blown my cover, and that I was under surveillance. You would not ask me to make an intercontinental trip to give me instructions on how to get out of the country. You would get the information to me while I was here in the United States, by having me call the KGB from a pay phone, or have one of their officers call me at work, or some other back-channel method. But they would never call attention to me by hauling me off to Europe for a face-to-face meeting.

It's standard procedure for the CIA and the KGB to "stand down," that is, temporarily suspend its local operations when some sensitive event happens or is scheduled to happen, such as a major scandal or the visit of a head of state. Yurchenko's defection on August 1, 1985 would have instantly triggered a KGB stand down in the U.S. A message would go out to all agents to immediately cancel all planned meetings and go "on ice" until they received further instructions.

When you recruit an agent, you develop these contingency plans in the earliest stages of contact. You get all the biographical information possible: where he lives, where he works, all his phone and fax numbers, and the phone numbers of his parents and relatives. Then you establish a danger signal for that agent. If I had been a KGB agent, they wouldn't have summoned me to travel all the way from New Mexico to Vienna and then sent me back. Some KGB illegal agent in Philadelphia or Tucson would have gone to a public phone, called my office and given me the danger signal.

Furthermore, if I were in Europe already when the fat hit the fire, the KGB would contact me there and say, "We want you to come with us right now. We'll find a way to take care of your wife and son. We'll send them money, or do dead drops, we'll have illegal agents in America visit them and put packs of money in their mail box, but you can't go back home, because Yurchenko has identified you."

In summary: If I had been an agent, the KGB would never have asked me to meet them in Vienna. And if I did go to Vienna after Yurchenko defected, the KGB would never have let me go back. And if I had been in Vienna after Yurchenko defected and insisted on returning to the United States, I would not have waited for an FBI investigation to get my affairs in order and get back out again. I would have left immediately. Why didn't I do any of this? It's simple. I wasn't a Soviet spy.

The only odd thing I recall about mid-August of 1985 was an unexpected visit from an FBI agent, Bill Gillespie. He said that he had a follow-up question to ask me about my official dealings with a man named Philip Troutman, a New Mexico state employee who had been indicted for trying to extort money from a New York bank. At the time, I thought it odd that Gillespie would come by in person to get information he could have obtained from me over the phone, but in retrospect, his mission was clear. Gillespie wasn't interested in Troutman. He had come to verify my residence so that the FBI could start my surveillance and install a telephone wiretap. He was part of what would become the FBI's sixty-man, twenty-four-hour-a-day Ed Howard surveillance team.

The FBI's hunt for evidence against me was on.

Chapter Six

Seeing Shadows

A green sedan caught my eye one evening while I was watering the yard of our small, adobe-style home. It was late August of 1985. My wife, Mary, would soon be calling us to dinner, and my two-year-old son, Lee, was playing near the garden. Except for the car, everything was normal.

We lived on a gravel street called Verano Loop in a community known as El Dorado, southwest of Santa Fe. I knew all of the neighbors and their cars, and this green car and its driver didn't fit in. It was driven by a young man wearing a baseball cap. As he cruised slowly past our house, he appeared to take more than a casual interest in me, and I wondered who he was. Was he looking for an address? Was he lost? Or was he a thief, casing the area for a future break-in?

Something intuitive clicked in my head and I jumped into my Jeep, calling to Mary that I was going to the store for a few minutes and that Lee was outside. I decided to circle around the opposite side of Verano Loop and see what the green sedan did.

Driving quickly, I made a left turn about a hundred yards from our house, and cut across the loop. Hopefully, I'd meet the green sedan coming from the opposite direction or see where he had stopped.

Within a minute my guesswork paid off: there he was, coming toward me on the opposite side of the loop. As we passed each other on the dusty gravel road, the driver of the green sedan tried not to take special notice of me, but the look on his face was one of anger. He was pissed. He knew he'd been burned.

I drove on, but my mind was full of questions. Who was he? Why was he interested in me?

My mind flashed back to the previous day, to a car that appeared to be following me home from work. I noticed it because when I stopped at a service station, it parked for no apparent reason about two hundred yards away. Were these two cars related? And again, why were they interested in me?

Only once before had I been followed like that. My stomach turned when I thought back three years before, when my wife and I were training for our Moscow assignment. We trained against surveillance teams of CIA and FBI officers in the Washington, D.C. area. When I thought about that, the memories of my CIA work, the grueling polygraph sessions and my forced resignation all came flooding back into my head.

"No, it couldn't be them!" was my first reaction. I had left the CIA over two years before. Besides, why would they care about me anymore? All that I knew about the CIA had either been forgotten or was obsolete by now.

At that point, I was ready to admit that I had been working too hard on oil price forecasts for the Legislative Finance Committee and that I was seeing ghosts. I thought, "Maybe the guy in the green sedan is just lost, or is someone just out enjoying a sunset drive."

My CIA training overrode my wishful thinking, however, and I also recalled one of James Bond's maxims: "Once is coincidence. Twice is enemy action."

I drove my Jeep towards the entrance to Verano Loop to see if the green sedan had stopped at our local ice cream store. He wasn't there. With a vanilla ice cream cone in hand

I chuckled to myself about the affair, but at the same time, I chided myself on not getting his license plate number.

I hopped back into my Jeep and started for home, but something kept nagging at me, and I knew that I had to make one more effort at flushing out the quail before I could put this escapade to rest and get a good night's sleep. Halfway home, I whipped my Jeep into a U-turn and headed for the Interstate Highway 25 entrance to El Dorado.

The El Dorado Wilderness Area was located about three miles away from the Interstate 25 El Dorado Intersection, so I bypassed the regular interstate and headed south on the Old Santa Fe Trail Road. About a mile down the road I turned right on a gravel road, under a bridge. As I did so, I noticed the green sedan and a gold-colored General Motors car brake as they went by my turn-off. Something was still not right.

I drove down the gravel road as it wound to the left and was obscured from behind by a hill. Once behind the hill, I again made a left turn onto a small dirt road and parked about twenty-five yards away, turning my Jeep to face the gravel road. I turned off my lights, and thirty seconds later, the two cars that were tailing me drove down the gravel road. As they passed, I turned on my headlights, temporarily blinding them. Then I headed down the dirt road for home.

I was angry and scared on the drive home. I felt like Butch Cassidy when he kept spotting the posse following him over impossible terrain: "Who are those guys?"

Again I cursed myself for not obtaining their license plate numbers. Their actions ruled them out as burglars, since burglars don't follow their targets around on dirt roads. They were clearly government agents—but if I wanted to make a case of government harassment, I would need better evidence.

Halfway home, and just past the entrance to El Dorado, I pulled one more provocative trick to verify what was happening. I turned my vehicle up a hilly dirt road that was tough going for cars but no problem for my Jeep. A third of the way up the hill, I parked and waited with my lights out.

I climbed out of my jeep and looked in the direction of the entrance road. Every minute or two I could see a car passing by, but I was too far away to determine the make. After about ten minutes of waiting, no cars had appeared to follow me up to my hiding place. Was I finally alone?

Nope. The answer to my question came from above. The distant drone of a light aircraft engine grew louder and louder above me. I could see his wing lights flicker as the plane circled my area. He continued circling my position at low altitude for at least five minutes before I climbed back into my Jeep and started for home.

From my CIA training I knew that the FBI used light planes and twilight scopes to track Soviet diplomats in the United States. The New Mexico state police had no reason to be mounting this operation. That left little doubt in my mind: the FBI was on my case. But why?

It obviously had to be connected with my previous employer. But although my resignation was not on the best of terms, there was no reason for the FBI to watch me now, two years later.

I arrived home late for dinner and told Mary why I was late. She took my story in stride and appeared not to be flustered. I think she thought I was either playing a joke on her or seeing ghosts.

"Oh, come on, Ed!" she said. "You must be seeing things in the dark. Do you remember how we used to think everyone in Washington was watching us when we really had no surveillance whatsoever."

"I know that," I said. "But why would I see the green car in three different places and then have an aircraft circle my position in the dark?"

"Let's see what happens tomorrow," Mary said. "Maybe you're right."

The next few days I was busy at the office. The Legislative Finance Committee was meeting just before Santa Fe's City Festival and everyone was concerned about the state's revenue picture. It seemed like my paid consultants were flipping coins about the future of oil and gas prices and those prices drove the bulk of state revenues. I had little time to worry about surveillance ghosts.

Early in September the city held its festival and filled with tourists. Sometime during this period I had another brush with surveillance. I left my office one afternoon and drove to a pharmacy. A light blue Mustang with a male driver caught my attention, so I took a round-about way on my return to the office. The Mustang followed discreetly on my return and stopped a block away when I parked near St. John's College. I took a short walk around an athletic field and got back in my car. Then I drove past the young man in the Mustang, who obviously had nothing to do but sit in a parked car in a place where he didn't belong.

I noted similar surveillance during early that month in downtown Santa Fe.

Mary asked if I was still noticing anyone, and I said I wasn't sure. She said she had noticed nothing unusual. We both felt that if the CIA had anything to ask me, they would call directly. They knew where to find me. They didn't need a back door approach.

I briefly considered calling the CIA to ask what they wanted, but knew that it would be futile. They would deny everything about anything, as I had been taught to do.

"Admit nothing, deny everything, make counter-accusa-
tions" was what they trained me. No, I would have to wait
for them to make their move. I'd have to go about my
business as usual and not let them rattle my cage. I had
nothing to hide, and hoped that sooner or later they would
leave me alone.

The weekend of September 14, 1985, I was scheduled to
attend an oil and gas conference in San Francisco. I looked
forward to the trip and planned to take Mary along, fly up
to Seattle and combine business and pleasure. My parents
agreed to come to Santa Fe and take care of Lee for five days.

That Saturday we flew to Seattle and rented a car with no
real objective other than to enjoy the Pacific Northwest. Our
first day in town was uneventful except for a marvelous
salmon dinner on the wharf. Sunday, Mary and I arose and
planned to spend the day enjoying a car trip around the
Seattle area before catching our evening flight to San Francisco.

At breakfast, I picked up the local newspaper and found
a front page story about Oleg Gordievsky, the KGB station
chief in London, who defected to the British. If it's true, I
mused, my old bosses must be having a field day.

After breakfast we set out on a half-hour car ferry across
Seattle Bay and headed south. We decided to take the long
route to the wildlife park in Kings County. Somewhere on
the road to the park, I noticed a light plane flying low around
the highway. The plane continued to circle the highway in
the direction we were heading for almost half an hour until
we reached our destination.

I became more convinced at that point that the surveillance was real. Even Mary, who had doubted it before,
became a believer. I'll never forget the eerie feeling we
shared watching the plane fly patterns above us. I had
always thought that airplane surveillance was done from

five thousand feet or higher. But this plane was barely a thousand feet above the highway.

At the wildlife park, I stopped the car near some trees, which obscured it from above, and we entered the main gate. After a short walk around some animal exhibits, we headed for the train which would take us on an excursion to see the park's animals.

Two young men in their early twenties with baseball caps stood as if to greet us when we walked up to the train station. They were not with a group, had neither girlfriends nor children, and stuck out like sore thumbs. The short train ride through the park was interesting, but my mind could not shake the sight of the small plane, the men and why they were there. The surveillance was not at all subtle, and I wondered why?

Mary and I caught our evening flight to San Francisco. Once settled at our downtown hotel, we walked to China- town for dinner. On our walk to the restaurant I joked with Mary about walking by the Soviet consulate, even though I didn't know where it was located. I figured my surveillance had been a little too pushy with their airplanes lately and I wanted to punish them a little with a twenty minute prome- nade in front of the devil's den.

"Ed, you can't be serious!" Mary scolded.

No, I wasn't serious, but the reactions from my baseball- capped friends would have been priceless if I had.

We flew home to Santa Fe on Tuesday evening. My father had already returned to Dallas and my mother was still in town taking care of Lee.

On Wednesday I returned to the office and accepted the usual envious teases from my co-workers about my business trip to San Francisco. Sometime that morning I received a phone call from Fred Johnson, my ex-CIA buddy from Texas.

Fred told me that an FBI officer had been snooping around his apartment complex that day, asking the apartment manager questions about him. When Fred confronted the FBI agent, he was told that a background investigation was being conducted. The agent refused to disclose any more and would not even tell him who was being investigated.

Fred had worked in Bolivia prior to his resignation from the CIA and was planning to return there in a month or so to investigate business opportunities.

"They must have picked up the fact that I've made plane reservations to La Paz and they don't want me to go back there in an unofficial capacity," Fred surmised.

I agreed with him that the CIA would not welcome having an ex-operations officer back in the same city with active agents still around, but I wasn't sure why the FBI would be involved in that case. I wanted to talk to Fred more about what was happening to me, but I knew the phone was no place for such conversations. Besides, what could he do but commiserate with me?

I drove from my office to eat a sandwich with my wife, now working as a dental assistant. On the way, I noticed the driver of the car behind me at a stop light. He was the same man who was on the plane with Mary and me during our West Coast trip. I was sure of that because when I noticed him on the plane I had remarked to my wife how much the man reminded me of an old friend and co-worker.

At lunch I told my wife about Johnson's call and my most recent surveillance observation.

"What are you going to do about all of this?" she asked me.

"I don't know what I can do, but this can't go on forever," I said. "Sooner or later they'll have to either confront me or give up these games."

I reflected on all of the times I had seen surveillance during the past three weeks and on Fred's phone call. Somehow I felt sure that everything was connected and that things would soon come to a head. I was right. Come to a head, it did.

Chapter Seven

La Trampa

"I'm Special Agent Jerry Brown from the Albuquerque District Office of the FBI," said a voice over the phone. It was 1:30 p.m. I was sitting in my office. "We would like to speak with you."

I asked what he wanted, and he said it would be better if I came to his room in the Hilton Hotel to discuss the matter. I suggested we meet the next day.

"I'm afraid this matter is too important to wait until tomorrow, Mr. Howard," came Brown's curt reply. "We would like you to come to the hotel as soon as possible."

I reluctantly agreed, told the receptionist I was going out for a while and walked the five blocks from my office to the Hilton.

On the way, I sipped a can of soda and watched the surveillance cars pass by me a couple of times. In the hotel lobby, two men stood up and moved toward me. One was large, wore glasses and appeared to be about fifty years old. The other was slender, tanned, about forty-five, with dark, beady eyes.

"Thank you for coming, Mr. Howard," said the larger man. "I'm Jerry Brown and this is Mike Waguespack, from our Washington counter-intelligence office."

I said hello and asked what I could do for them.

"It would be better if we went to our room to discuss things," Waguespack took control of the conversation.

We ascended to a room on the second floor. Agent Waguespack asked me to sit down while his colleague stepped out to get something. The room was a normal deluxe hotel room—with one exception. Instead of tourist information about Santa Fe, a map of Vienna, Austria was laid upon the coffee table. I sat while Waguespack stared at me.

Within three minutes, Jerry Brown reappeared with a third man. I recognized him immediately: George Morgan, my former boss from the Soviet division of the CIA.

I always had good feelings for George and I greeted him with surprise and warmth. He cut me off. "You can discuss any matter with these men here today that you would have discussed when you were working with me in Washington." I asked George what it was all about, but he said it would be better left to the FBI agents.

George left the room. Jerry Brown locked the door behind him, and Mike Waguespack's eyes continued to glare at me. Then it began.

Waguespack held up a recent copy of the *Washington Post* with the story of Oleg Gordievsky's recent defection to the British.

"Did this news story bother you?" he asked sarcastically.

"No. I read it in Seattle and found it interesting, but it didn't bother me."

"Well it should have," Waguespack snarled, "because this man has named you as a KGB informant."

I was amazed, but at least the meat was on the table now. After weeks of cat-and-mouse surveillance games, they had finally confronted me. I reacted with a low-key chuckle. "So that's what this is all about. No, I'm not a KGB informant. I'm just a man trying to forget you guys and what you did to my life."

Waguespack was not pleased. "Look, why don't you just tell us what you've been up to and rest easier. We know all about it anyway."

"No, no, no! You're wrong!"

"Yes, we're right!" said Waguespack, while Brown shifted position in his seat. "We know you went to Austria in September of 1984 and met with the KGB."

"That trip is no secret. My expenses are all on my American Express card. Why should I hide anything about the trip? I went with my family to an economic conference in Milan and then drove to Munich via Austria for the Oktoberfest."

Waguespack showed me a photo of a man with German features, gray hair in a light-colored trench coat. "Have you ever seen or met this man?"

"No, not to the best of my knowledge," I answered.

"Okay. Then will you take a polygraph test today to confirm you're telling us the truth?"

"Are you serious?" I was incredulous. "You destroy my life and CIA career with polygraph tests and now you want me to take another one? Hell, no, I won't take one. I try not to make the same mistake twice."

Waguespack wasn't happy with the way things were going, and he started to bully me with threats. "We're going to get to the bottom of this, with you or without you, and we won't give up until we do. We can make your life hell on earth here in Santa Fe. We will question your employer, your friends, neighbors, and family. Even your son!"

"My son is only two years old," I told him. "And before you start making allegations which you can't prove, you'd better think twice, because I'll get a lawyer and sue your ass off!"

I was mad and knew that I had better cool down, but the statement about involving my two-year-old son got my adrenalin going and I wanted them to know that I was ready to fight.

"Why do you need a lawyer?" Brown interjected. "They only screw things up and cost you money." He was trying to calm the situation.

"I still have some rights left," I told them. "Before I talk any further with either of you I want to consult with a lawyer. You say you want me to tell the truth, but I know how you guys operate. You may take your families to church on Sundays but you all have one thing in common. You are all hypocrites, you lie, and you never bat an eyelash while you're doing it."

"Something has probably gone wrong someplace in Langley, and you want to use me as the scapegoat. Well I won't fall for it. Go find someone else to blame for your troubles."

"Get yourself a lawyer," said Waguespack. "But it won't change anything. We are proceeding on this case without any delay. How long will it take you to get back to us with your lawyer?"

I told that I had a major presentation before my committee the next day and it would be Monday before I could consult with a lawyer.

"That's not good enough," said Waguespack. "If you don't get back to us by tomorrow we're going to interview your boss and co-workers at the legislature."

(I later found out that the FBI started interviewing my boss that very same afternoon.)

I agreed to contact a lawyer the next day. I stood up and moved toward the door. Jerry Brown stood between me and the door. "Remember, we start tomorrow, Mr. Howard," said Brown, turning to unlock the door.

Déjà vu. Again I stood accused with no evidence. But this time I'd get a lawyer and fight these guys.

I phoned Mary from my office and told her about my confrontation with the FBI. I assumed my phone was tapped, but it didn't matter to me anymore.

"What! Are you serious?" Mary was shocked.

I told her I'd be home soon. I tried to concentrate on my work but gave up after fifteen minutes. As I drove home, my surveillance came into the open. The light blue Mustang followed me and a dark GMC truck drove in front of me all the way to El Dorado.

When I reached home I saw my wife and mother taking Lee for a stroller ride near the front of our house. I also saw another FBI car drive up. A middle-aged man and a husky, younger woman were inside. They stopped beside me and the male driver asked, "Mr. Howard, we'd like to interview your wife for a few minutes."

"She's over twenty-one and can do as she pleases," I said.

The FBI pair approached Mary and led her about a hundred yards down Verano Loop while I went inside the house with my mother and son.

I telephoned Morton Simon, a lawyer I knew in Santa Fe, and told him the events of the afternoon.

"Tell Mary I don't recommend talking to the FBI until we find out more about their allegations," said Morty. "Come see me tomorrow at one o'clock."

I went outside, climbed into my Jeep and drove to where Mary was standing with the FBI agents. From behind, another FBI car saw me heading toward them and proceeded to overtake my Jeep at a high speed. He whipped into a U-turn facing my Jeep, putting his car between me and my wife.

I stopped my Jeep, climbed out and shouted to Mary that Morty said it was better to talk with him before talking to the FBI.

"Your wife just told us the same thing, Mr. Howard," said the older FBI agent.

Mary and I went back into our house and pondered the situation. We were both nervous.

"They've finally let me know what it's about, but I'll be damned if I'm going to be their fall guy," I told Mary.

"Isn't there somebody you can call to help you?" she asked. I told her that a good lawyer was the best step, and that I certainly wasn't about to confide in anybody back at Langley, where the whole mess was originating.

Later that evening we all drove into Santa Fe, and stopped at a Safeway store to buy groceries. Their surveillance was not discreet and stayed with us for the entire round trip. Perhaps the most unnerved person of all was my poor mother, who had never before experienced such harassment.

She asked what it was about and whether I thought I would go to jail because of it. I told her the truth about the interrogation, but assured her that I was a long way from going to jail. I suggested she return to Dallas to tell my father about the possible ordeal ahead.

I had a difficult time falling asleep that night. About midnight I got up and walked into my back yard. It was raining lightly and I slipped on my poncho in order to walk the grounds, about an acre and a half. As I walked in the dark I heard noises from the neighbor's yard behind my house. Never before had I seen a camper parked there, but there it was, the source of the noise.

More surveillance, static as well as mobile. Bless my neighbor's heart for allowing the FBI to shadow me! I thought how the FBI must have told him it was a matter of "national security" for them to use his land. If he was like everyone else in Santa Fe, the poor guy probably just said, "Yes, Sir!" and saluted.

That's how they'll work this case in Santa Fe, I thought. It was a small town full of intelligent but provincial people who would be easily swayed by claims of "national security." That excuse would convince neighbors to cooperate and would probably be enough to get judges to issue search and arrest warrants.

In New York or Los Angeles, people might question the men from Washington and their national security claims, but not here. I felt that the deck was already stacked against me, and I had little faith that our local judicial system would deal fairly with me.

I knew that even if the FBI couldn't prove the espionage charge, they could keep me in jail for several months waiting for my case to be heard, and that alone would ruin my career with the New Mexico state government. After I beat the espionage case, I'd be out of a job and the allegations would linger. Acquitted car thieves can always find some sort of work but acquitted spies can never hold a government position again.

And then there was the probation terms. If I were even convicted of bed-wetting, that alone would be enough for the state to revoke my parole and lock me up for more than seven years.

It was at that point that I seriously began to consider escaping.

Escape? With full-time static and moving surveillance?. And to where? With limited funds and the responsibility to support a wife and small son?

The next day, Friday, I went to work with surveillance cars in front of and behind me. My mind was not on my presentation to the Legislative Finance Committee, but on my upcoming duel with the FBI.

Mary had driven my mother to the Albuquerque Airport that morning and was to meet me at the lawyer's office in Santa Fe at one p.m.

I left my office at noon, stopped at the bank to withdraw a few hundred dollars in case I needed it, and drove to my lawyer's office.

"They tried to interview me again at the airport," Mary said, "but I told them I wanted to talk with our lawyer first."

"Did you have surveillance to and from the airport?" I asked.

"Yes. But on the way back I took the old dirt road through Galisteo and there was so much rain they couldn't follow the Jeep." Mary laughed.

"Good going." I gleefully pictured the heavy, FBI sedans vainly attempting muddy roads in a heavy rain. It was nice for little David to claim at least a temporary victory over Goliath.

We explained the situation to Morty Simon. When I told him I was being followed and that I thought my phone was tapped, his reaction was not inspiring. "Great," he said. "That means your call to me yesterday gave them my telephone number and now my phone is probably tapped."

And lawyers wonder how they got bad names. The Feds want to put his client in jail and he's worried about his phone. After listening to the basics, Marty told us I would need a specialist in federal criminal law. He recommended a female lawyer in Albuquerque.

Afterwards, Mary and I went food shopping. At a local supermarket I surprised one of my tails by walking up to him. I told him to tell Jerry Brown to come by my house about five or six that evening. The young man from the light blue Mustang approached me in the supermarket about five minutes later with the message that Mr. Brown wanted me to call him. I found a pay phone.

"We'd rather have you come by our hotel room, Mr. Howard," said Brown.

They probably had a tape recorder there, I thought. Nonetheless, I agreed to meet them later that afternoon.

After Mary returned to El Dorado, I roamed around town in my Jeep. I didn't want to meet the FBI until late in the business day, and besides, it made me feel good to keep them waiting. As I cruised the streets, I carefully looked for car escape points in case I wanted to elude surveillance. My spy training was coming back to me.

At four o'clock I went to the hotel. As I approached Brown's room, a group of four or five young men scattered. I recognized them as my surveillants.

Jerry Brown and Mike Waguespack had nothing new to say. They asked if I was ready for a polygraph test. I told them that I was retaining a lawyer in Albuquerque, but that we had not been able to reach her. They asked for her name and telephone number, which I gave them. Waguespack reached for the room telephone and dialed the Albuquerque lawyer's number. When it answered, he gave me the phone. It was the lawyer's secretary, and she told me that her boss was out. I left my name and said I would call back on Monday.

The FBI agents were not happy with the delay until Monday, but I was glad to have the weekend to mull things over. On Monday afternoon I was scheduled to fly to Austin, Texas on business, but I promised them I would attempt to visit the lawyer before I left. I gave them the flight information for my Texas trip and told them I was going first class courtesy of a frequent flyer bonus.

"I hope you won't find it necessary to send your boys first class, too," I joked. "It would cost the taxpayers a lot of unnecessary money."

Brown and Waguespack didn't appreciate my humor. They scowled.

I hadn't yet decided whether to escape or stay to fight the charge. The FBI, I now know, planned to arrest me the following Monday.

I drove home from my meeting with the FBI and had a quiet dinner with my family. Afterwards, Mary and I put Lee to bed and took a walk around Verano Loop. I told Mary about my options. As I saw it, I could stay and fight the charge, but would probably spend months in jail and lose my job. Or I could escape and decide later what to do.

"What good would escape do?" Mary asked. "They'll always pursue you and you'll never be able to live here again."

"What good would jail do?" I responded. "I can always elect to come back and fight the charges. Even though flight would make me appear guilty, at least I'd have some time to think and see how the case developed. Perhaps they'll find someone else or keep quiet about the whole affair. No one knows what the future holds. Besides, if I go, I'll be taking most of the mess with me, and maybe the FBI will leave you and Lee alone."

We walked around Verano Loop several times that night, debating the pros and cons of staying or escaping. After a while, it seemed futile to stay and fight.

I told Mary that if the FBI and CIA came into the small, conservative community of Santa Fe and told the judge that I was an alleged Soviet spy and a flight risk, he would not hesitate to lock me up on a probation violation. At least one of my trips to Europe had been a probation violation, and that alone could keep me in jail for up to seven years.

"I can't win against these guys in Santa Fe. They have no proof, and you know that I'm not guilty, but they're going to go to the judge on Monday morning and I'll be in jail by Monday afternoon."

That would be the government's ace in the hole: even if they could never convict me on espionage charges, they'd have the satisfaction of seeing me in jail for seven years because of my probation violations. Given the option of seven years in jail or flight, I chose flight. It was a simple choice. Back then. Now I wish I had remained and fought them. They had nothing on me. I probably would have been jailed for a few months to a year, and the charges would have been dropped for lack of evidence.

When Mary and I arose the next morning, we scouted around for surveillance escape points. In my CIA training I learned a tactic we called the "jack-in-the-box" (jib) jump routine. It was devised to evade surveillance in Moscow. You find a place on the road where your car temporarily disappears from the view of anyone following you. At that point, the passenger jumps out of the car, leaving behind a pop-up dummy in his place. If done properly, the surveillance doesn't detect the switch until the jumper is long gone.

That morning Mary drove into town with me in the front passenger seat wearing a baseball cap. I wanted surveillance to become accustomed to my wife as the driver and for them to also become familiar with my baseball cap. We chose a carefully planned route to scout sites I thought would be good jib escape points.

First we proceeded to my office to drop off some clothes and an overnight bag hidden beneath my raincoat. Then we spent an hour in a shopping center, my drive-in bank, and a pastry shop. All typical Saturday morning stops. In the course of making these stops, I pinpointed several target sites for my jib escape.

We returned home around noon and examined each site on my map. Mary and I went out into the back yard to discuss the merits of each, assuming that our house had been bugged.

By mid-afternoon I made up my mind to escape. I told Mary that I might be gone a few days, weeks, months or even up to a year, but that our families would take care of her and to have faith in our reunification. I had no idea of where I would go, but it would be better if she did not know my destination anyway.

Mary had tears in her eyes, but said that she understood my reasons. I only hoped that my prediction would come true: that I would be taking the whole mess with me and that she and Lee would be left in peace.

I fabricated the jib dummy at home on the morning of my escape. It was a crude but effective dummy, made from a sawed-off broomstick with a coat hanger for the shoulders, my wife's styrofoam wig holder for a head, and a disguise wig I had left over from my CIA training. The jib was dressed in a beige, Calvin Klein field jacket and a solid-color baseball cap.

I wrapped the jib dummy in my raincoat, took it into the garage, opened the car door and put it into the footwell on the passenger side of the car. I also disconnected the brake lights, so that they would not flash when we slowed down for the jump.

I decided that dusk would be the best time to escape and that we should use a trip to town for dinner as our cover for the jump. Mary called a babysitter to come by the house at half past five and we set about planning the affair in detail. The jib jump was scheduled for seven-thirty.

I spent my last half hour at home playing with Lee and chatting quietly with Mary. I told her to expect some initial harassment from the FBI if I escaped, but that she should get a good lawyer to fight them if they persisted. After all, I reasoned, their fight was with me, not with her.

I had a last-minute brainstorm which, I hoped, might buy me some additional time. I made a tape recording of my voice, and the plan was that if everything went well and my jump wasn't detected, Mary could call Dr. Dudelczyck's answering machine and play my taped voice over the phone. My taped message said that I'd see him again next week. It was designed to give the FBI phone tap operators reassurance that I was still at home and keep them off my trail. It evidently worked.

The babysitter arrived and I had to say good-bye to Lee. He seemed to sense something was wrong and started to cry. After hugging him one last time I walked to the car, my own eyes streaming with tears. I got into the passenger seat, put on my baseball cap, and Mary drove us to Alfonso's, a piano bar on Canyon Road.

On the way, we were amazed to find no surveillance, and we wondered where on earth they were. I wanted surveillance to see us go into town and come back so that they would not come snooping around my house before Monday when I was due to start work. You get an eerie feeling when you expect surveillance and you don't see it. You like to know where your tails are. At the restaurant we ordered hors d'ouevres, but we were both too tense to order main dishes. Our surveillance had still not shown up, and I was worried.

I came up with an idea. Knowing that my home phone was tapped, I had Mary go to the phone and call the babysitter. She told the sitter that Lee had suffered a slight fever that day, and that we were at Alfonso's on Canyon Road and could be reached at such-and-such a phone number if needed.

Within ten minutes, the FBI tail's car cruised by the restaurant, and a few minutes later, a blond agent with glasses came in, went to the bar and ordered a Coke. He looked at me, and I looked at him, and I thought, "Okay, he's here, I'm back in control."

We rose, I put on my baseball cap again and got into the passenger seat. Mary drove. We headed from Canyon Road towards Old Pecos Trail. Mary took a wrong turn and I swore a couple of words, but immediately felt ashamed. I probably wouldn't see Mary for a long time, and I had been focusing entirely on my escape—completely ignoring her dilemma and feelings. I was watching my wristwatch, noting the sunset, rehearsing the execution of my jump, the exact route, the distance between our car and the tail car— scores of details. But I was ignoring the important part: that I was leaving my wife of ten years, the love of my life, and in a few hundred yards, I had to jump.

Back at Camp Peary, Mary and I had practiced the jib jump over and over again under the watchful eyes of the instructors, who yelled and screamed at us until we got it right. Now was the moment of truth.

We neared the junction of Canyon Road and Old Pecos Trail, near St. John's College in Santa Fe. This was where the road dipped, turned to the right, with substantial hedges planted along the right side. As we came up to the jump point, I turned and looked at Mary. Her face was serious, and her eyes were moist with tears. Our marriage and our love were both on the line.

"Goodbye, babe," I said, and Mary slowed to five miles an hour. I moved to the outboard side of the seat, flipped up the dummy, put my hat on it, opened the door, jumped out and shoved the door closed as I jumped. I tried to hit the ground running but landed hard and rolled into the bushes.

It was to be nineteen months before I saw Mary or Lee again. Much to the amazement of us all, our reunion would be in Moscow.

Chapter Eight

Run for Your Life

My arm throbbed with pain as I scrambled to conceal myself behind a large hedge. From my hiding place I watched Mary continue down the road, satisfied that the pop-up dummy did its job. My escape and evasion instructors from the Denied Areas Operations Course at The Farm would have been proud of me. A strong rivalry exists between the CIA and the FBI, and the Agency always relished beating their FBI counterparts—as I just had.

Within a minute the young FBI tail in the sport coat from Alfonso's restaurant drove by. He did not slow down, but appeared to speed up in an effort to close the gap between himself and Mary's car. I waited in the bushes another five minutes to, then set out at a brisk jog to my office in the state capitol building.

First I gathered the clothes and overnight bag I had sneaked in earlier that day. Then I typed a letter of resignation to my boss, Phil Baca, citing personal reasons and requesting that all my salary and pension funds be given to Mary. Finally, I wrote a hasty good-bye note for Mary, which I put in a separate envelope along with my resignation letter. I tried to make it sound like she was unaware of my escape plans. I hoped that she would be able to tell the FBI that I went for a mountain hike and didn't come back. I left the letters on Phil Baca's desk.

These tasks took about fifteen minutes and it was nearly 8:00 p.m. when I ran out of my office to catch the airport limousine at the Loretto Hotel three blocks away. As usual, the airport limo was late. I boarded with one other passenger. I cursed to myself when I remembered that the limo made one more hotel stop before leaving Santa Fe: the Hilton Hotel, where the FBI interrogation and surveillance team was headquartered! The driver opened the car doors and we waited in front of the Hilton for about five minutes—an eternity to me as I slumped nervously in the back of the limo. No other passengers boarded and the limo finally drove off. I heaved a sigh of relief and continued to watch for surveillance.

The limo arrived at the Albuquerque airport shortly after 9:00 p.m. I called home, but by prearranged plan, I said nothing to Mary when she answered. If my escape had gone undetected, she was to answer normally; if my escape had been detected, she was to answer in an irritable voice. Her answer was normal, but I could detect a great deal of emotion in her voice. I owed her much credit for my escape. Weakened by the emotional encounter, I hung up and moved on quickly to the airline counters.

I thought there would be a 9:30 Southwest Airlines flight to Dallas, but my information was out of date. Instead, the only plane leaving that night was a United Airlines flight to Tucson, which I barely made. I still had no idea about my ultimate destination. I knew only that I wanted to be a long way from Santa Fe.

The flight to Tucson was nearly empty. At Tucson airport, I paced the airline counters for almost an hour studying my options. There were no more flights that night, so I focused on departures the following morning. But where to?

Mexico? No, that was too obvious, too much a cliche.

Miami en route to South America? I still had friends in Costa Rica, Colombia and Peru.

Europe, where I had once lived as an adolescent?

I couldn't decide, but checked into the airport hotel to think things through.

After a light meal and a couple of beers, I went to my room and played with red hair dye I'd bought earlier that day in Santa Fe. Ultimately, I decided it would draw more attention to me than it would disguise my appearance.

I used my room phone to call several toll-free airline reservation numbers and finally made a reservation with TWA to Copenhagen via New York. "Why not have some fun?" I said to myself. I had never been to Copenhagen, and I knew the FBI would start their search by checking all my previous residences. It was late—nearly two a.m.—before I went to sleep.

I presented myself early at the TWA counter for my eight a.m. flight to New York and Copenhagen. I reserved a business-class seat and charged it to my TWA Getaway credit card. I chuckled about what the FBI would think when they saw my Getaway card invoice.

TWA had no business-class service from Tucson to New York, so they gave me a first-class seat. I boarded early, anxious to get out of the departure lounge where I could have been identified. A tanned, silver-haired gentleman took the seat next to mine and I immediately recognized him as Lee Marvin, one of my childhood heroes.

I was too shy to make conversation with him. I stared out the window as we flew east over New Mexico to St. Louis. My thoughts were with Mary and Lee, down there somewhere.

About an hour out of Tucson, I started *The Hunt for Red October*, which I'd bought at an airport newsstand. Lee Marvin eyed the paperback.

"It is a pretty authentic piece of writing," said Marvin. "Look up front and check out all the places he got his information."

We chatted about the book and our travel plans. He was bound for Israel to make a movie; I said I was flying to Copenhagen for business. It took my mind off my troubles for a while, and I'll never forget meeting my hero from *The Dirty Dozen*. I asked him for his autograph and he signed a blank postcard.

During our brief stop in St. Louis, I mailed the postcard to Mary. It was later confiscated it by the FBI—a memento, I like to think, of my escape.

We arrived at Kennedy Airport in New York just after five. These were anxious moments—I feared the FBI could already be wise to my escape. I later learned that Phil Baca had come in to the office on Sunday evening. He called the FBI when he read my resignation, and by 9:00 p.m. on Sunday —when I was already halfway to London—the FBI knew that I had resigned. Hours later, they knocked at Mary's door and discovered I had gone.

At 6:30, my flight to Copenhagen departed from New York. Airborne again. I breathed a sigh of relief. This time, on my way over the Atlantic, out of the country. But still unresolved was this question: where do I hide?

I arrived at London's Heathrow Airport before sunrise. The plane refueled, departed, and we arrived in Copenhagen at 10 a.m. on Monday morning, September 23.

I decided on the spot that it would be unwise to stay in Copenhagen since I had used a credit card to buy my ticket. I still possessed about three hundred dollars in traveler's checks. So I decided to go further east, to Stockholm or Helsinki.

I didn't go through customs in Denmark, but remained in the international area and bought an S.A.S. ticket for Helsinki. It was mid-morning and I had two hours to kill before my flight. I sat and drank coffee to help recover from jet lag.

In Helsinki, a customs agent eyed my Levis and hiking boots and asked how long I intended to stay in Finland. "Ten days," I replied.

Paranoia had been setting in since I awoke in London. I walked into the arrival area and sat down to think. It was about 3:30 on Monday afternoon, Helsinki time, early Monday morning in Santa Fe, and there, the FBI surveillance team would be waiting for me to leave the house for work. If they didn't see me appear by mid-morning, they'd check the house personally, and my number would be up. I needed help and at least a place to hide while I could think things over rationally and figure out what had happened back home. There was only one group of people who would truly welcome me, but I was afraid of them. They were, of course, the Soviets.

I knew that the Soviets would relish the opportunity to talk with a former CIA officer from the Soviet division. What I didn't know were the answers to questions like these: What could they offer me in the way of refuge? A hiding place in Finland or in the Soviet Union? And would they ever let me go?

I decided to take a chance. I could at least talk to them, feel them out. I would be under no commitment, but I could see what they might do.

I hailed an airport taxi and told the driver to take me to the Soviet embassy. He didn't know where it was, so we stopped at a phone booth to find the address. A few minutes later he dropped me off at a building with a Russian sign in front. I paid the fare and entered the building.

I had forgotten most of the Russian I'd learned in Washington, but I was able to determine that this was not the embassy, but some sort of trade mission. The receptionist told me that the consulate was further down the street.

It was near closing time when I arrived at the Soviet consulate. I introduced myself and said I wanted to speak to a consular officer.

An officer came immediately. He was about fifty years old and very fat. He asked me what I wanted and I told him the story of my FBI surveillance and interrogation in the U.S.A. My greatest fear was that he'd think I was some kind of kook and have me thrown out onto the street. I gave him my regular tourist passport, and, to add some credibility to my account, I handed him Jerry Brown's FBI business card.

His initial response was cool and cynical, but he took my passport so that he could make a photocopy. He left me alone in the reception room and came back a few minutes later with another man. He was also about fifty, with grayer hair and glasses. I was asked to repeat my story.

"You must understand that we know nothing about you and we must cable Moscow for their opinion," said the man with glasses. "What is it that you want from us?"

I told him that I wasn't sure, but that I needed a temporary place to hide or at least some advice on which countries to hide in. "I'm not sure if that means I want to go to Moscow or not, but at least we can talk things over," I added.

The officer suggested I check into one of two hotels downtown so they could find me after cabling Moscow.

"It will probably take a couple of days to get a response," he said.

I didn't think it was going well; I felt that they were treating me like some kind of crank.

I didn't think Helsinki would have to wait long to hear from Moscow. Soon after processing a name trace on me, the

Soviets would undoubtedly come up with this kind of information from the KGB computer:

☐ From our consul in Washington, we know that Edward Lee Howard, U.S. diplomatic passport # X186527, was granted a multiple-entry diplomatic visa on May 18, 1983, to serve as second secretary at the U.S. embassy in Moscow;

☐ From our communications intercepts, we know that Howard was to be a deep-cover CIA officer whose assignment was canceled at the last moment; and

☐ From the same source, we know that he was very angry at being fired from the CIA.

I was a tired, jet-lagged traveler and I took a taxi to the first hotel the Soviets suggested.

A receptionist told me the hotel was full, and I returned to the street with my bag. I had no idea where the second hotel was, but there was a pleasant-looking one about a half block away. They had a room—and I was soon asleep.

I awoke in the early evening and walked to a nearby Greek restaurant for dinner. I did some further thinking about my immediate future. My situation was ironic. Three years before, I'd been planning to go to Moscow as an enemy intelligence officer, and now I was praying they would help me. From some deep recess of my mind I recalled the Arabic saying, "The enemy of my enemy is my friend." I wanted to explore my options with the Soviets, if only to satisfy my curiosity about what they would offer.

The next morning I arose early and took a sauna, just what I needed to help clear my head and relax my nerves. Later, in the hotel lobby, I signed up for a bus tour of the city. It would help kill time while waiting for the Soviets to make up their minds.

My funds by now were dwindling. I checked out of the hotel in hope of finding a pension—a less-expensive inn—later in the day. After touring Helsinki for three hours, the bus driver dropped me at an inn he suggested by the waterfront. I checked in, had lunch, then visited the Soviet consulate to see if they had any news.

I was greeted by a young man who appeared glad to see me. He led me to the reception room and ordered a soft drink for me. Within a couple of minutes, the older consular officer with glasses appeared.

"Where have you been staying?" he asked. "We checked both hotels looking for you."

Moscow had sent Helsinki a blistering cable, chewing them out for not making me comfortable—and keeping me on Soviet territory—while waiting for a decision. I later learned that they had turned Helsinki upside down looking for me.

"Moscow would be glad to receive you at any time, but we must act quickly to get you out of the country," he said. "You can stay in an apartment here in the embassy until we make arrangements, and you'll be safe in the meantime."

I told him I would accept his hospitality at the embassy, but that I was not yet sure about traveling to Moscow.

"We can discuss that later," he assured me, "but first you should check out of your hotel and get your bags here."

I agreed. He sent an embassy car and driver with me to the inn. I checked out and returned to the Soviet consulate, where I was led to a spacious apartment, complete with kitchen facilities. The consular officer told me to rest for a couple of hours while they communicated with Moscow about my situation.

In the late afternoon he returned and told me Moscow thought Helsinki was unsafe for me, and that I should leave that night for the Soviet Union. I agreed—providing that everyone understood I was going to Moscow to hide and that the matter would be kept secret, plus I could leave the Soviet Union whenever I desired. The Soviet official agreed, with the condition that I sign a statement that I was going to the U.S.S.R. voluntarily, and for my own protection. I signed the statement, adding in my own hand that I was to be allowed to leave the Soviet Union when I desired.

We discussed my travel arrangements to the Soviet Union. Three consular officers—two men and a woman—and I would drive to the Finnish-Soviet border at Vyborg. Just before we reached the border, I would be hidden in the trunk of the car and remain there until we were several kilometers inside the Soviet Union. The two male consular officers would get out at the border checkpoint to present the diplomatic passports of the three persons legally crossing the border, while the female officer would remain in the back seat of the car. This was to appear to be a courtesy to her, but the real reason she was to stay in the car was to provide search dogs with a human scent from inside the car.

I gave the Soviets my U.S. diplomatic passport. They stamped two entrance visas onto it. They made a mistake on the first one, and they voided it; the second one was dated September 24, 1985. The visas were for the Finnish border guards in case I was discovered. I don't know how they planned to explain why I was hiding in the trunk of their car, but that was their problem.

We left Helsinki about 4:00 in the afternoon and traveled east on the highway that parallels the Gulf of Finland, a finger of water which is part of the Baltic Sea. It took us about two hours to drive the one hundred miles to the frontier. Just after we passed Virojoki, a small Finnish border town, they pulled over and helped me climb into the trunk. I was worrying about asphyxiation, but the driver assured me I was in no danger. "How does he know?" I asked myself, and wondered how many times a year they did this kind of thing.

The car started up again and we drove another mile or two to the border. The car stopped. I heard the doors open. I prayed that I wouldn't hear any barking dogs, but after what seemed an eternity the doors of the car closed again and we drove onwards for about a hundred yards. We stopped again at what I presumed was the Soviet border post and went through the same routine. When we left I expected them to immediately pull over and let me out. But they drove for about five minutes before stopping.

I climbed out and was welcomed into the arms of a tall, elderly man with a mustache and glasses. He wore a black derby hat.

"I am General Vitaly Alexandrovitch," he said. "I welcome you to the Soviet Union."

Chapter Nine

The Welcome Wagon

I tried to think of something momentous to say to General Vitaly Alexandrovitch, but all I could manage was, "Thank you for your help in coming here." The General introduced me to his aide, Vladimir, then ushered me into a black Volga. They were taking me seriously.

"We will travel to Leningrad tonight and then to Moscow tomorrow," said the General. "But first let's go down the road a ways. You must be hungry and we will have something to eat."

The silver-haired General sat in the front passenger seat; Vladimir and I sat in the rear. I never found out my principal escort's real name, but I did discover that he was a general in the KGB and he had been called off leave to supervise my exfiltration from Finland.

We pulled over to a hotel run by Intourist, the government-owned tourism agency. The restaurant was closed, but the General had a few words with the manager and he opened part of the restaurant for us. The meal was simple, and the General presented a bottle of Johnny Walker scotch to toast my arrival.

"We are glad to see you here and we will do everything to make your stay a pleasant one." He raised his glass.

I thanked him in my almost-forgotten Russian and drained the scotch. After a second drink, we set out on the long drive to Leningrad.

We stopped once in a small town for the General to make a phone call and report our progress. As we drove, Vladimir and I chatted in English; the General kept his silence in the front. Vladimir gave me a large picture book of Leningrad; I gave him my copy of *The Hunt for Red October*.

Vladimir asked about my family and my situation in the United States. I recounted the events of the past week. General Alexandrovich seemed to think that I was giving Vladimir too much information. He suggested that we try and get some rest. I took the hint and tried to doze as the car bored along into the dark, Russian night.

We arrived in Leningrad in the early hours of Wednesday morning, and drove directly to a large, well-guarded house. Despite our early arrival, an attractive brunette hostess greeted us and led us inside. She showed me to a suite on the second floor, then bid good night to Vladimir and the General, who slept nearby. She said I would be called for breakfast at about nine in the morning. After that, a flight to Moscow.

I couldn't sleep. I was concerned about my family in New Mexico. What was happening to Mary and Lee? I had two sets of parents to look after them, but still I asked myself, had I done the right thing for them by escaping? Certainly, the focus would be off of the family and on me. Maybe the FBI would be too embarrassed by my escape to proceed with the case.

The hours of this night passed slowly. Finally, at eight, I arose and showered. I marveled at my suite's beautiful wooden furniture and at the extensive, well-manicured grounds and gardens surrounding the house.

I walked downstairs to a dining room and was greeted by the hostess. She offered me fruit juice. Then Vladimir appeared. He suggested we walk around the garden until the General was ready to join us.

At nine, General Alexandrovitch appeared and invited us to breakfast. The elegant table was set with a lavish selection of eggs, meats, caviar and vegetables. The General offered me a drink, but I declined. I wanted to be in full command in Moscow.

"That's good," he said. "We have a new campaign against alcoholism in the Soviet Union and we usually don't allow drinking before two in the afternoon."

The General laid out our travel plans: We'd catch a plane for Moscow at 11:30. I would be given time to rest before sitting down to analyze my situation. He asked if I had any special requests to relay to Moscow. I had none.

Our black Volga raced through the streets of Leningrad to the airport. "Why does this chauffeur always drive like maniac?" I wondered. "Aren't there any policemen around?" Vladimir pointed out interesting sites that we fleetingly passed.

Upon reaching the airport, I was ushered into a conference room with Vladimir while the General checked on our plane.

"I won't be going with you," said Vladimir, "but I wish you luck—and I hope that you see your family soon."

The General returned and directed me to join him in his car. We drove onto the runway to an Aeroflot plane already full of passengers. I said goodbye in Russian to Vladimir. The General and I boarded the plane. A flight attendant ushered us to the last two seats in the rear of the plane and I took the window seat. General Alexandrovitch had asked me to avoid speaking English on the plane, so it was a quiet hour and twenty minute flight to Moscow.

The whine of the jet engines had barely quieted at Moscow's Sheremet'yevo International Airport when a large *Chiaka* limousine pulled up to the plane.

A flight attendant announced, "Everyone stay in your seats until you are told to get up."

She came back to us and escorted us to the front exit.

At the bottom of the ramp we were greeted by a friendly-looking, middle-aged man who introduced himself as Igor. I soon learned that he was Colonel Igor Anatolyivitch Batamirov, Chief of the American department of the KGB's counterintelligence service.

Igor grabbed my arm, shook my hand and said, "Welcome to Moscow, Mr. Howard." He motioned me to the waiting *Chiaka*. General Alexandrovitch said goodbye to me. He said he hoped we would meet again soon.

Inside the limo, I joked with Igor about how nice it was to be able to avoid going through customs.

"You're luckier that you avoided the FBI," he quipped.

"Yes, thanks to my wife," I said.

"You will be together with your wife and son soon," said Igor. "If we announce that you are here, your family can join you in a matter of days."

"No! No! We agreed that my presence here was to be kept secret. I can't come out in the open in Moscow now. It would destroy my family."

"Yes, we agreed and we will keep our word, but you must know that the only safe way to see your family will be with our protection. The FBI will never let you return to them without passing through their jail."

As we drove south on the Moscow Ring Road, Igor tried to calm me down and told me not to get too upset about things.

"Time is on our side, and you are safe now. I'm sure that you are right. Your parents and your wife's parents will take care of your wife and son for now and we will work to get you all back together soon."

We were headed to Yasenevo, the headquarters of the First Directorate (intelligence) of the Soviet KGB. The headquarters of the First Directorate is a government complex roughly the equivalent of the CIA's headquarters in Langley, Virginia. Unlike Langley, which is hidden in dense stands of trees, the tall, towering buildings of Yasenevo are easily visible from the Ring Road.

We entered Yasenevo from a narrow, unmarked road off the Ring Road. A hundred meters down the quiet, heavily-forested road is a simple "No Entry" sign. Those who blunder past the first warning come face to face—300 yards later—with a heavily-armed guard post. This marks the perimeter of Yasenevo, the Holiest of Holies of Soviet intelligence.

Our *Chiaka* was motioned through the gates into the compound. We drove past the tall office building to a light-colored brick house surrounded by a wooden fence eight feet high. A well-dressed guard in civilian clothes opened the gates and our *Chiaka* continued on into a small parking area. I climbed out of the limo with Igor.

As we entered the house, another well-dressed man greeted me with a youthful smile. "Hello and welcome. My name is Sasha."

"His name is Ivan Ivanovitch," (the Russian equivalent of John Smith), interrupted Igor, introducing me. "Please help him get settled."

Sasha led me into the house and introduced me to the cook, a jovial, chubby lady named Galinina. The house (known as a *"dacha"* or country house) was cozy and comfortable. It had two bedrooms, a dining room, a study, a kitchen and a good-sized living room. A large wildlife painting hung behind the sofa. I took the last bedroom at the end of the hall, as Sasha had already placed his bag in the smaller bedroom. The *dacha* was temporary living quarters for visiting officials.

"First we would like to have a doctor check you over if you don't mind," said Igor. "You've been through a lot and a short medical exam would be to your benefit."

I agreed. A middle-aged female physician arrived in my bedroom minutes later for an examination. Igor translated while she listened to my heartbeat, checked my eyes and throat with a small flashlight and tested my reflexes with a rubber hammer. The exam was over in ten minutes and she told Igor I appeared normal and in good health.

Igor and I sat down for a chat.

"So far everything is still quiet about your escape from the U.S.A.," he said. "General Secretary Gorbachev was informed about your arrival this morning, but we will honor our word and keep your presence here secret for the time being."

"It's going to be hard to keep secret the fact that I left the United States," I said.

"Yes, they know that, and they're probably breaking doors down everywhere to find you. But we must at least try to keep them in the dark for now. We were discussing every possible option and contingency at the office this morning. Can you give me your passport, coat and a set of your clothes?"

"Yes, but why in the world would you need them?"

"They are thinking of faking your death to throw the FBI off your trail. We may decide to send one of our officers on a sea voyage. Your clothes and passport would be found, giving the impression you were washed overboard and drowned." Igor said this with little conviction. "Anyway, we're still working on many ideas."

Igor told me to prepare for lunch. He said a special guest was coming to welcome me. I was tired from jet lag and lack of sleep, but I tightened my tie and combed my hair. Christ,

I was thinking, they don't even give you time to think around here.

The lunch guest was a short, plump man with glasses in his mid-fifties. He was introduced to me as General Anatoly Tihanovitch. He was accompanied by General Alexandrovitch, who had escorted me from Leningrad. We sat down to a lunch of hors d'oeuvres, caviar and chicken.

At the start of our meal, General Tihanovitch rose to toast me. He mentioned my family, promising that all would be fine in due time. I thanked him and expressed my gratitude for all their help in bringing me to safety.

During the meal they asked how I had escaped from the FBI. *"La trampa,"* I replied, and of course that drew puzzled expressions from all of them. I explained that *"la trampa"* came from the Spanish expression, *"hacer la trampa,"* which means to play a trick on someone, or to con them. I told them about the jack-in-the-box trick—how my wife and I used our CIA training to elude the FBI. They were fascinated by the trick, but they refrained from asking any more about tradecraft at that time. They knew that getting me settled and analyzing my immediate problems were top priority.

As we finished lunch, General Tihanovitch asked if I wanted or needed anything. I requested a short wave radio so I could monitor world news.

"You will have one tomorrow," said the General. "And also copies of the *International Herald Tribune, Time* and *Newsweek* as soon as we receive them."

The generals departed and I was left with Igor and Sasha for the afternoon. We talked mostly about what could be done to help my family. I wanted Mary to know that I was okay, but not to know where I was. Igor asked me where she would be and how she could be contacted.

I told him that she and Lee were probably at her sister's home in Minnesota by now, and I gave him her sister's telephone number. Igor left me with Sasha and promised to come back the next day.

Sasha and I spent the rest of the afternoon chatting about my life in the United States, and he compared it with his life in Moscow. We talked about pay levels, prices, cultural and recreational opportunities, just like a couple of foreign students in a college dormitory. Later, we played poker, using strips of paper as chips, and drank a couple of beers before dinner. I felt like I was back at college.

I arose next morning and jogged around the perimeter of the *dacha* fence. Galinina made breakfast and Sasha introduced me to two Russian dishes: *blini* (Russian pancakes) and *tworug* (similar to cottage cheese).

Igor came back in the late morning to talk and have lunch with us. He told me that there was no news about me yet and delivered a short wave radio sent by General Tihanovitch. We talked more about getting a message about my safety to Mary.

Igor said that someone could call her and tell her I was okay and not to worry about me. I was worried that the FBI would take action against Mary in revenge for my escape, but reasoned that letting me jump from her car was not a crime, since there was no warrant for my arrest in force at the time. I approved Igor's plan and we worked on the contents of a message together.

That night, after a round of poker and dinner, I listened to the short-wave radio in my room. Sasha popped his head in after I'd been listening to "Voice of America" and asked about the news. "No news about me," I said. "We have an expression in English that 'no news is good news.' "

The days wore on and I grew accustomed to my daily routine. First exercise, then news, breakfast, Igor for lunch, walks in the *dacha* garden and dinner. All the time, Sasha and I traded information about life in our respective countries, jokes, and we played poker and black jack. I taught Sasha solitaire.

Late Saturday, Igor told me that they had placed a telephone call to Mary and that we would have a tape of the call within three days.

"Yes," said Igor with a smile. "She's apparently okay and sends her love to you, Ed."

So far so good. But such good vibes weren't to last.

After lunch on Tuesday, Igor took me for a walk in the garden and he quietly revealed the first hint of bad news.

"Washington is quite upset about you," he said. "The FBI officers who normally watch our embassy in Washington are now seen visibly displaying their guns."

This meant, it seemed, that they did not know where I was and that they thought I might attempt a dash into the Soviet embassy. They were still looking for me and had not yet announced my escape.

I heard even worse news on Wednesday morning from "Voice of America." They spoke of a worldwide manhunt for me and that I was suspected of espionage. The VOA even played an interview with Phil Baca, my boss at the Legislative Finance Committee in Santa Fe. He said he was totally surprised by the charges and described me as "a quiet, hard-working individual." That was to be the last nice thing I heard about myself in the media. I listened hard for any news about Mary. There was none.

I became anxious and depressed. I thought first about my family; not only Mary and Lee, but also my parents and sister. What they must be going through!

I was angry with the CIA. I had done everything those bastards had asked me to, and here they were on my case again, harassing my family as well.

Alarmed by my reaction to this news, Sasha telephoned Igor to come over. He appeared within the hour and tried to calm me down. He told me to focus on the positive news: that my wife was okay and with her family, and that I was safe.

"There's no news about her helping you escape, and she's okay," Igor assured me. "We'll have that tape tomorrow to prove it. In the meantime, you should be calm and prepare yourself for more bad news. The CIA will undoubtedly start a disinformation campaign to assassinate your character and make you look guilty."

Igor was right. The next day VOA broadcast that I had been dismissed from the CIA for drug use. During the next few weeks I was called everything from traitor to thief to alcoholic to womanizer. One of my new-found colleagues in the KGB asked me what "womanizer" meant. When I told him he joked that they'd call me a homosexual, too, except that it would conflict with them calling me a womanizer! I chuckled at his joke, but it only concealed my hurt inside.

I knew where it was coming from: Corridor 2-D at Langley, where the press section of the International Activities division was located. I had a friend there who told me how journalists and publishers could be persuaded to print the "correct" story.

Later that afternoon Igor stopped by with the tape of the phone call to my wife. I rushed into the study with a cassette player and listened to the short call. A male voice gave her my message that I was okay and loved her and my son, and she responded emotionally to the message. Mary told the caller that she and Lee were okay and that she loved me. The messenger did not identify himself nor give any indication of my whereabouts. He simply stated that he was my friend, played a short tape in my voice which assured Mary of my love and concern, and recorded her answer.

I became emotional and excited when I heard her voice. Igor came back to the study and told me he had some more good news. "Tomorrow you are going to have an important guest for afternoon tea. General Vladimir Aleksandrovitch Kryuchkov would like to visit you and see how you are."

"Well, I don't know who he is, but if he's a friend of yours, he's welcome."

"He's in charge of the KGB's First Main Directorate (the intelligence division) and he's interested in your welfare."

Next day, after reading periodicals and running through my morning routine, I sat down to lunch alone with Sasha. We had been together for over a week and had developed a good rapport. I remarked on how well he was dressed that day. Sasha smiled.

"Vladimir Aleksandrovitch does not come to my house often," Sasha chuckled. "I have only seen him once when he was addressing a very large conference."

"Okay, I get the hint," I said. "I'll put on my only sport-coat and tie. Does he play poker?"

"You should not joke too much, Ivan Ivanovitch. He's a very serious man."

I was intrigued by the impending visit and tried to imagine what it would be like. "He'll probably be tall and over-weight and have a couple of guards with him," I thought. "Then he'll slap me on the back a couple of times, drink some cognac with me, and ask me to remember everything I learned back in the CIA."

At 3:30 Igor appeared and said my guest would arrive within the half hour. He began to chain smoke and appeared nervous. I asked him what was up and he said that the meeting was important for my future and he wanted me to be serious and calm.

Was this Darth Vader himself I was meeting with, I wondered. What was the worst he could do? Kick me out of the Soviet Union? Stop me from listening to the "Voice of America"?

Promptly at 4 p.m. a car pulled up at the *dacha* gate and three men got out. They came into the house and Igor introduced me to General Kryuchkov. He was neither tall nor fat, but a bit shorter than I and trim. He had gray hair, his eyes twinkled with the vitality of a younger man. My eyes fell to his black boots and I mentally nicknamed him, "Dickey boots."

General Kryuchkov introduced me to the other two men with him. Colonel Vladimir Ivanovitch Mechulayev, the first, was silver haired with an athletic build. He spoke excellent English. The second man, Colonel Victor Ivanovitch, was the tallest. He was balding and possessed sharp Germanic features.

We all sat down around the dining room table. Igor interpreted for us. The General ordered tea and cookies and began our chat by welcoming me to Moscow. I thanked him for his welcome and remarked on the professionalism his people showed in getting me into the Soviet Union.

"They were not very professional at all, and I have already reprimanded them for that," Kryuchkov exploded.

All of the men at the table were quiet and I now knew why Igor had been so nervous beforehand. Although small in size, the General had a dominant personality and the tenacity of a terrier. "They should never have turned you out from the embassy the first day," the General boomed. "They should have made you comfortable for a few hours while they cabled for instructions. You are very lucky that you are safe."

General Kryuchkov went on to explain that Igor, Victor, Vladimir and I would be working together as a team to analyze my situation with the twin objectives of keeping me safe and reuniting me with my family.

"I have been told how important your family is to you and we will do everything we can to get you back together again. In the meantime, you must have patience and work diligently with my men to achieve that objective." The General's eyes were softer now.

I told the General how much my impression of his service had changed in the nine days I had been inside the Soviet Union.

"To be honest, I thought I might just be locked up in a safe house and interrogated," I told him.

"We do not all wear black hats," he replied.

(Later on, I asked Igor what Kryuchkov meant by this. Igor said that he was probably referring to Sergei Yurchenko, the famous double-defector who had allegedly fingered me as a CIA mole. Igor had attended KGB basic intelligence school with Yurchenko. Igor said that Yurchenko had a sponsor on the Central Committee of the Communist Party who kept getting him promoted despite his "basic lack of intelligence.")

"We will see that you are made more comfortable than being stuck in this small *dacha*," said Kryuchov. "You need to get out and see some of the cultural attractions of the Soviet Union and enjoy some sports activities as well. Soon you will move to a new *dacha* and have the opportunity to visit theaters, museums, and go skiing when the snow arrives."

The General said that since there was a worldwide hunt on for me, he was sending a cable to all his officers stationed abroad to be "on the lookout for Howard as he might be of possible interest to the KGB." He said the cable would leak to the Western security services and thus serve to protect my true whereabouts. This was practically an admission by the KGB chief that his service had been penetrated, but I was grateful for his efforts to protect me, and I said nothing.

The General, Victor, and Vladimir departed, and I was left alone with Sasha and Igor. Igor told me to work with Sasha on the list of places I would like to see while he checked on our new living quarters. Igor also said that because I was in the Soviet Union "black" (undisclosed), I would need a disguise for moving around town.

"We did okay today," Igor said. "Vladimir Aleksandrovitch is really interested in helping you."

Kryuchov was not the Darth Vader that the CIA taught me to expect. There was no talk of information, only about my family and my personal situation. So far, everything was the opposite of what I was taught to expect by the Soviet division of the CIA. Even Sasha, my beer-and-poker buddy, was not what I had expected. He also had a family, and he talked about the same things I did when I talked of my family: schooling for his children, his wife's attitude about beer drinking, the commuting time to work and other concerns.

My CIA training had led me to believe that the Soviets were the embodiment of all that was evil. President Reagan himself spoke darkly of the "Evil Empire." The KGB was portrayed as the agency that beat up our officers, slashed our automobile tires and ransacked our apartments. I'd been left with a negative impression of the Soviet Union, its people, government and especially the KGB.

But my KGB contacts had been far more hospitable than I had ever imagined possible, and they were not trying to squeeze information from me. Instead, they talked only of getting me settled and back together with my family. I was aware that their hospitality could just be a ploy to seduce me into cooperation, but for now I was relieved, if not content.

I drafted a cultural activities plan for my next couple of months in the Soviet Union. Sasha talked excitedly about the

Bolshoi Theater, the Pushkin Art Museum, the Kremlin Palace, a trip to Leningrad to see the Hermitage Museum and other trips to Kiev, Georgia and Volgograd.

For the next ten days I had to remain in the small *dacha* at Yasnova until a larger one was prepared for occupancy. Sasha stayed with me the entire time, except for Saturday afternoons, when Igor came to relieve him so that he could be with his family.

Victor, Vladimir and Igor brought me American periodicals, and we continuously reviewed what was happening back in the United States. The Senate Intelligence Committee was holding hearings on my case. More character assassination data was being leaked to the press about me. But there was no word about my wife, except when *Newsweek* published an article stating that Mary and Lee were still waiting for me in El Dorado.

We took a team approach to my case. Igor was at the helm, but we all contributed our ideas about what could be done. We tried to analyze what the FBI was doing to my family in the United States, and how we could learn more about them. Most importantly, we focused on the problem of covert communications with Mary. We assumed that she was under full-time surveillance; that the house was bugged and the phone tapped. I learned a lot about counter-intelligence from Vladimir and Victor.

The daily routines of exercise and poker continued, and served as a safe way to blow off steam while we waited for news and analyzed events. Someone must have gotten tired of seeing me wearing the same three or four sets of clothes all the time, as they brought me a bundle of new shirts, pants, and a couple of new suits.

Three weeks to the day after I first arrived in Moscow, Igor announced that my new *dacha* was ready. I would move in the next day. It was brand new, and I was to be its first resident. I was excited to finally leave my "golden cage" at Yasenevo into more spacious quarters.

Chapter Ten

The Golden Safe House

My new *dacha* was near a small town called Veshki, about a half-hour drive from downtown Moscow. We approached it down a narrow, paved road and stopped at a green gate. A guard peered through the gate and allowed us in. Three uniformed guards saluted and we drove toward a large, Scandinavian-style, one-story brick house.

A mature blond woman appeared at the door and welcomed us inside. Inside the large entrance hall, a glass door led to a spacious, modern living room with a fireplace. Off the living room to the right, a dining room furnished with ornate Hungarian furniture. To the left, a study-cum-solarium with windows overlooking the woods. Adjoining the solarium, my bedroom, large and tastefully furnished in a European style, plus a bathroom.

The house had a guest bedroom with bath, a large kitchen, servants quarters and a small office for the hostess. It was a handsome residence with extensive, wooded grounds, surrounded by a high fence.

I was introduced to the hostess and cook as Ivan Ivanovitch. Igor proudly showed me a small refrigerator and bar, stocked with German beer, tonic waters, Coca-Cola and fruit juices.

We took a tour of the *dacha*'s grounds—ten acres of pine and birch trees. An alarm went off in the distance.

"They have some sort of light beam shooting across this end of the area," Igor pointed to a metal device sticking out of the ground.

We then returned to the house as another car drove up. I greeted Sasha and Vladimir and we all went into the house for lunch.

The food was superb and was served in grand style by our hostess. Caviar and smoked salmon, followed by a hearty soup, and a meat dish. Dessert and coffee rounded out a perfect meal. I was amazed by the quality of the food, and I was told that it came from a special storehouse—the *Politburo baz*—which served only *Politburo* homes. We even had bananas, a rare treat inside the Soviet Union.

Vladimir told me not to worry about my weight. "We'll jog, ski and get plenty of exercise," he said. "We know that you've been through hard times and deserve some time off. Enjoy yourself now. Later, sports will help you relax and stay trim."

Sasha spent the first night with me in the new *dacha*. We felt like two kids in candy store. We listened to Billie Holiday records on the stereo and drank beer. As diplomatically as I could, I asked him whether I would be permitted to live by myself in the future.

Sasha said that Igor felt I should not be left alone for the time being. He said that he, Victor, and Vladimir would take turns staying with me until I felt adjusted—if I didn't mind. I said it was all right, as long as they understood that I wanted to be left alone in the study or solarium at times.

What they didn't say was why. They knew from experience what I did not: Many defectors never make a good adjustment to their new lives, and several had committed suicide within the first three years after their defection.

After the first few months of my unofficial presence in Moscow, my KGB guards at the *dacha* saw that I was becoming extremely depressed, especially when I had to spend Christmas alone without my family. In the spring of 1986 I was introduced to Dr. Boris Ivanovitch, a psychiatrist whose specialty was hypnotherapy.

Dr. Ivanovitch used hypnosis to help me deal with the stress and frustration I was experiencing—the worry for my family, and having to witness the maligning of my character without the opportunity to defend myself. He taught me the basic techniques of meditation: controlled breathing, visualization exercises and relaxation techniques.

A new routine soon evolved. It consisted of morning exercise, breakfast, listening to the news on short wave radio, walks, lunch, reading and a light supper. The cook and hostess would arrive each morning at nine and depart at 3 p.m. The cook prepared a light meal, which we'd enjoy at about 7 p.m. while watching television.

It was during this period that the KGB intelligence professionals debriefed me. It is known in the intelligence business that the value of knowledge decays quickly, and it had been almost two and a half years since I had worked for the CIA. The KGB found out just how true this was when they asked me questions about alleged CIA officers and procedures.

Technically, anything that I knew that was stamped Confidential, Secret, Top Secret or above was classified information. Transmitting any of that information to a foreign power would leave me open to prosecution. So that leaves open the question, What did I know or divulge to the Russians that was "hard data?" The Russians knew about my work long ago. They learned nothing new from me.

A classic example of data I would have been able to relay was pictures of people I had worked with, and I'd be able to say, "Yes, that was Tom Jones. Yes, that was Bob Smith." I was shown pictures, and I think that for 99 per cent of the pictures, they already knew who the subjects were. Maybe they were testing me. Maybe they were hoping that I knew the one out of a hundred they didn't know.

I did not give the Soviets any names or descriptions of Soviet or American human assets, nor tell them anything about operations in Moscow that they did not already know. In short, I gave them nothing that would endanger the security of the United States or its citizens. And to the claims that I caused "tremendous damage" to CIA operations in Moscow and "closed them down over there," my answer is this: Those statements may have helped sell some newspapers and books, but they have no basis in fact.

The Soviets were interested in the attitude of CIA officers toward recruiting "hard" versus "soft" targets. For the CIA, hard targets were potential agents from the Soviet Union, China, Cuba or any diplomat from a socialist country. "Soft" targets are target recruitments of citizens from the rest of the world, particularly Latins and Africans.

Foreign intelligence operations officers get turned on when they confront their toughest competition in conflict, the same way that Harvard MBAs get turned on by corporate takeovers or Navy Seals get turned on by landing in a hot landing zone. Nothing charges the blood more for a CIA officer than pitting him against the KGB and telling him to recruit at will. In this case, the KGB officers were hardly in combat with me, but they had an ex-CIA officer in the same room with them, and it was obvious that they were enjoying this immensely.

I must say that I enjoyed fielding these types of questions because they were easy and I was not giving out classified information. They could have learned anything I told them by watching a few James Bond movies or reading John le Carré novels, but it was more interesting to get it from the "horse's mouth." Me.

Another question I was frequently asked centered on the control procedures for CIA recruitments. The Soviets were interested in the restrictions placed upon the CIA officer by Langley and his local chief of station. Who could he or she attempt to recruit? When could they attempt recruitment? What notification or approval procedures would have to be followed between the officer and his superiors before recruitment? What types of monetary or non-monetary promises could be made in attempting recruitments? These questions were quite general and not related to any specific operations. Previous books about the CIA gave them the general answers to these questions but the procedures are really not all that hard and fast, nor are they always followed by every CIA officer.

In practice, recruitment can follow different lines. At Camp Peary, the CIA had a legendary recruitment instructor who I will call Tom. He was a legend in the Agency because of his prodigious record of recruiting agents in Germany during the Cold War. Tom's most famous lecture at The Farm was known among the students as the "toilet pitch." Tom was a beer lover with an obvious distaste for bureaucrats and regulations. The "toilet pitch" lecture, which described his quickest recruitment ever, was his way of showing it.

Tom was in a bar in Hamburg one night when a slightly-tipsy East German started complaining about life at home. Tom worked his way down the bar and got next to the man. They engaged in bar chatter, and he found out that the man was an East German official on a short business trip to West Germany. Tom would ask his wide-eyed audience, "Do you think I had time to draft a cable to Langley and have some smart S.O.B. in CI (counter-intelligence) second guess me on my instincts?" When the East German excused himself to go to the men's room, Tom followed and made the quickest recruitment on record. While standing next to him at the urinal, he passed him contact instructions for his next trip West!

One question the Soviets asked me still sticks out in my mind. It related to "false flag" recruitments by the CIA. A false flag recruitment is when an agent is recruited by an intelligence officer and the agent does not know the real country the officer is working for. For example, the CIA might use a Hispanic-American officer posing as a Mexican national to recruit someone from El Salvador. There are a number of reasons that a CIA officer might use a false flag recruitment. The target might not like America, or the CIA might want to cover its tracks if the agent went bad and informed his government. The Soviets were interested in knowing whether this type of recruitment was a common practice for the CIA. My answer was that I did not know, due to my limited experience.

The reason this question was posed to me is revealing, and only after a couple of years here did I really begin to understand why it was asked of me. The Soviets were almost totally paranoid about the United States and the CIA. They viewed both as the source of many of their problems at home, as well as abroad. I suspect that when they unmasked agents who supposedly were working for the Germans or French, they had suspicions that it might be some sort of CIA false flag operation.

Besides questions about general recruitment procedures, I was asked questions about CIA training for new officers, agency personnel policies (including my old nemesis, the polygraph) and the relationships between the CIA and other U.S. government agencies such as the NSA and the State Department. I was continually amazed by these routine questions, the answers to which could have been easily found in any number of published books on the CIA.

I was also posed questions about CIA information priorities. What types of information were considered most critical? What was the National Intelligence Priority List? I had never seen this kind of document while working for the CIA. Like everyone else, I knew the obvious choices. The CIA is interested in any penetrations of its own service, in threats to the national defense, foreign military capabilities, foreign political developments, and so on. I learned all these things in my U.S. National Security Politics course when I was a junior at the University of Texas in 1971.

Victor summarized the KGB's debriefing of me in four words: *"Bolshoi golova, nyet informatsii"* (big head, no information). This became a standard joke after the first couple of days of debriefings. I didn't mind. I didn't come to the Soviet Union to give them information. I came for protection from my persecutors. My *dacha*, apartment and comfortable life here was not paid for with information. It was given in return for the propaganda value of finally having a former CIA officer living under KGB protection in the Soviet Union —after seeing so many of their own go in the opposite direction.

I've never felt bad about not having information to turn over to the Soviets. I told the KGB when I arrived that I would never do anything to hurt "my people" in America, and I haven't.

Within a week of my arrival at the new *dacha*, Igor visited again and introduced my Russian language tutor. Her name was Anna. She was an attractive, tall blonde in her mid-twenties. Her personality was quiet and serious. Anna began my first lesson with the basics, even though I had once been fluent. She visited me two or three times a week. I was glad to have another young person to talk to, and her quiet, gentle manner reminded me of my wife.

Although the KGB made a disguise kit for me that included a beard, mustache, and glasses, Igor suggested that
I grow a beard, and I agreed. The first week or so I looked
like a Mexican bandito, but my beard finally grew in and
looked fairly nice.

Two major events took place on October 27, 1985. It was
my thirty-fourth birthday, but more important, a phone call
was planned to my wife.

Igor came to me a week before my birthday with news
from his generals. I had hoped that they would sneak me to
Vienna or another western city so that I could place the call
myself, but my KGB friends decided that would be too
dangerous.

"Every policeman in the West is looking for you," Igor told
me. "Even our own people don't know you're here, because
Vladimir Aleksandrovitch sent a cable to all KGB resident
agents to be on the watch for you."

Instead it was suggested that I make a short, taped message to my wife and the call would be placed by someone in
the West. They also suggested that I postpone any further
contact with my wife until things cooled down. How long
would that be? "Sometime next spring" was what Igor
suggested.

I felt frustrated and I became very emotional. I had always
planned to get back to my family in a few weeks or a couple
of months, but the KGB was now asking me to wait until
spring—and they were only talking about a lousy phone call,
not a reunion.

Igor and I debated the phone call options for a couple of
hours. He was sure if I left the U.S.S.R. to make the call I
would be caught. Returning covertly to see my family was
out of the question.

"Time is on your side. Be patient and you will win," he
kept repeating.

My rational mind told me that he was right, but my heart told me that I could not wait that long. How would my wife and son feel without me home for Christmas? I wanted to rush to them by Christmas and sneak into the United States with all of the Christmas travelers. On the other hand, I had told my wife to be prepared to be separated for up to a year. I had to trust that our families were taking care of them, pray for their safety and wait.

I compromised with Igor and decided to send a message that all was fine with me and that they would hear from me again in March of 1986. I made an emotional, one-minute voice tape telling Mary that I was okay and how much I loved her and Lee, and that I was praying for them. I ended the tape with the date and time of my next phone call in March.

Igor took the tape and departed. I sat in my bedroom, depressed and wondering how my wife would react to this news. I was still starved for information about her well-being.

Just before my birthday, the press reported that I had been sighted in Helsinki and that U.S. officials speculated I might have crossed the border into the Soviet Union. I was not surprised as I had used my regular tourist passport to check into the Helsinki hotel. Igor told me that the Americans had not yet officially asked the Soviet Union about me.

On October 27, my birthday, I invited the whole team to my *dacha* for lunch: Igor, Sasha, Victor, Vladimir, and Anna. The cook did a special job, treating us to a gourmet's delight, complete with cake and ice cream. I received several birthday presents, including my own short wave radio, sent by Vladimir Aleksandrovitch. I remember the day well because I kept thinking about the phone call that was being placed to Mary.

Igor and I discussed the phone call and my future plans over coffee and cognac. He told me that we should have a cable the next day confirming that the call had been made, and that the tape of my wife's response would arrive in another three days. In the meantime, Igor said, I should devote my time to planning more cultural excursions and think about how, where and when I could possibly meet with my family in the spring. I agreed to work on both plans, and spent the rest of my birthday relaxing with my friends and playing with my new short wave radio.

Next day, Igor sent word to me via Vladimir that the phone call to Mary had been made as planned and that she sent her love. I was very happy and relieved to hear this, and eagerly awaited the tape of her response. It arrived a few days later, and I rushed into my study to listen to it privately. Mary's emotional response upset me. She told me that she loved me but that she and Lee needed me very much and wanted me to come home soon. I could tell that she was practically in tears as she spoke. She acknowledged the next phone call date in March, but she didn't sound at all happy.

I immediately dove into planning how I could return to my family, writing Igor page after page of proposals on how it could be done. Meanwhile, I worked on my Russian with Anna. We spent a couple of hours several days a week on my language training, and I spent the rest of the day playing cards or chatting with Sasha or Vladimir.

I showed Anna my family photos and she commented on how cute Lee was. It was nice to hear that from her, because I knew that she was sincere. She was a language teacher, and not a part of the intelligence community like all my other friends. Her attitudes were a breath of fresh air.

I remember once, after finishing a session, Anna and I examined an American newspaper together. It contained an article about Soviet propaganda, and I said I hoped she wouldn't take offense by it. "I don't," she said. "The Americans make propaganda, too."

To their great credit, Americans are trusting people, and most believe that what they see and hear in the media is, or at least strives to be, straight-forward reporting of the facts. Few people in Des Moines, Iowa know that the CIA has an entire International Press office whose sole job is to twist, distort and manipulate the news media and the information they distribute. The KGB does exactly the same kinds of things, of course. And both agencies lie because their governments tell them to lie.

My frustrations over the reunification of my family boiled over that October. I had been in my new gilded cage only a week when I had my first confrontation with my KGB caretakers.

I had been waiting for Igor's response to my reunification plans for five days. After breakfast I asked Vladimir how Igor was coming with my plans. His reply was something along the lines of, "these things take a lot of time."

I had heard that line many times before, and this time, it set me off on a tirade. "What in the hell are you guys doing! My wife and son need me, and all you guys want me to do is plan a trip to the Moscow Circus!"

"Now calm down, Ed," said Vladimir. "You know we can't plan an international rescue mission in a few days. Besides, we have every indication that your family is okay. Be patient. Time is on your side."

"The hell with patience," I yelled at him. "I have to do something more than just sitting here, playing cards with you. There's a time for thinking and then there's a time for action."

Vladimir was seriously worried. He called Igor, who promised to come over quickly. When he arrived, we went to my study. Igor smiled at me and pulled a large, white-and-red pass from his briefcase.

"Do you know what this is?" asked Igor.

"No," I answered. "How does it affect my plans to see my wife and son?"

"It's a dignitary pass. It will enable you to sit near our leaders at the Great Revolutionary Parade on November seventh." It was obvious that Igor felt this was a great honor.

I was underwhelmed. "That's nice, Igor. I'm honored. But have you reviewed my plans to sneak me back to see my family, or to get them over here?"

Igor said he had, but that we needed more time. My wife was probably under full-time surveillance, her phone was tapped, and we had no plan on where to go even if the KGB could get them out of the country.

I tried to respond to each of the problems, but I knew that Igor was right in most of what he said. As unbearable as it was to be separated, the best thing for me to do was to wait. I agreed to go to the parade. But I told Igor I wanted to meet my family soon after January first.

"If they have her under their control as you suspect, then they won't be expecting me until March, and I can make my move in January," I told him.

Igor frowned, but I resolved to keep pushing him until something happened.

On the morning of November seventh, 1985, Vladimir and Victor took me to Red Square, by the Kremlin. I was in full disguise, because we would be in the stands with all the VIPs and diplomats, and my presence in Moscow was still secret. We took our seats to the side of Lenin's tomb and waited in a light snow.

Red Square is one of the most impressive sights in Moscow. The massive, brick walls and imposing towers of the Kremlin form one side of the huge, half-square-mile plaza.

The senior government officials review the troops and pre-side over the parade from atop Lenin's tomb, centered aside the Kremlin's outer wall. At one end of the great plaza is the ornate cathedral of St. Basil, with its famous, multi-colored, onion-shaped domes; at the other, the History Museum, and opposite Lenin's tomb and the Kremlin is the grand, old GUM department store.

The parade itself, with all its troops and tanks and missiles, was impressive, but after more than two hours in the cold I was ready to go home and drink hot chocolate. Vladimir said in earlier days, everyone brought a flask of cognac to these events, but that now it was frowned upon, due to the anti-alcoholism campaign.

Later that week I had another surprise. Victor Mik-hailavitch Chebrikov, the chief of the KGB, came to my *dacha* for dinner. Igor had a bad cold that day, so Victor and Vladimir did the translating for General Chebrikov and his colleague, my friend, General Vladimir Aleksandrovitch Kryuchkov, who accompanied him.

General Chebrikov opened the conversation by telling me about the vast territory and cultural resources of the Soviet Union. "Why would anyone think that we wanted more territory?" he asked. "You must get out and see our land and meet our people face to face. You will see that they, like you, are a peaceful people."

I told him that I would welcome the opportunity, and seized upon his visit to press for more excursions outside the *dacha*.

"I see no problem with that," he replied.

I smiled at Victor and Vladimir, who knew that this meant more work for them.

"See everything for yourself. Talk with whomever you want, but don't jeopardize your security," he added.

We had a pleasant dinner, and afterwards, I reflected on what Chebrikov said to me. He seemed genuinely concerned for me and my welfare. He talked of reunifying my family, and the importance of family values. There was no talk of intelligence matters, although he had heard how I escaped from the FBI and asked me how I made the jib dummy. The dinner with Chebrikov had chipped yet another flake off the monolithic, Stalinist impression previously ingrained in me about the Soviets.

Through November I went on cultural excursions downtown and visited the museums, the theaters and the Moscow Circus. Vladimir made arrangements for us to play tennis and have a sauna every Wednesday evening at Moscow's *Dinamo* Sports Club. I enjoyed the saunas and looked forward to cross-country skiing when the snow was deeper in December.

On Thanksgiving Day we had another feast and the cook made stuffed turkey with cranberry sauce, just like home in New Mexico. The whole team came over and we had a small party. Igor told me that my trip to Kiev had been approved for the following week and asked who I wanted to accompany me on the trip.

"Sasha and Anna," I replied. Igor told me that one of the KGB colonels should also go along, so I told him it didn't matter—either Victor or Vladimir would be fine. He left after the party and I expected that I would soon be touring Kiev with Anna and Victor or Vladimir. I was wrong.

The day arrived for my trip to Kiev. Sasha had said that he would not be able to go, but Anna was excited, as she had not been there before. At noon on the day we were to take the night train to Kiev, Vladimir, Igor and a guest came by for lunch. They introduced me to Larisa, an attractive Eurasian woman from Tashkent, who spoke English moderately well. She was about twenty-five years old with long, dark hair and an athletic figure. She had a happy-go-lucky nature but wore heavy glasses, which did not suit her. She had lunch with us and then chatted with the cook and hostess while Igor, Victor, and I took coffee in the living room.

"She's a very smart girl but needs more experience with her English," Victor said. "We would be pleased if you could help her out from time to time."

"Sure. No problem," I replied. "I'll give her some lessons after we get back from Kiev."

"We thought you wouldn't mind if she went to Kiev with you, Victor, and Vladimir," Igor said softly.

So. It was all decided: I was going to Kiev without my friends and with a complete stranger. At first I was angry, but I reasoned that they were paying for the trip, and by that time, I was anxious to travel anywhere. I made a last-minute plea to Victor, but the plan had already been made, and he went to get Larisa so that she and I could have a chat.

Larisa said that she felt awkward about being thrown into the trip, but I told her that I would welcome her company. I reasoned to myself that it wasn't her fault that Sasha and Anna weren't going, and I tried to be pleasant to her.

Our train left Moscow's Kievsky Station at midnight. It was snowing as I stared out of the compartment and waved good-bye to Igor. I was sad to leave him, Anna, and Sasha even though I had known them only two months. The train carried us off into the night and I looked at Larisa and smiled. She smiled back, and giggled nervously. Having her along wasn't a tragedy, I concluded. She was certainly attractive, and I had never met anyone from Central Asia before. I wished she wouldn't giggle so often, but I realized that it was probably her way of releasing nervous tension.

I found out later why Larisa seemed so nervous. Like Anna, Igor, Victor and Sasha, Larisa was part of the KGB's "Ed Howard Team," with one big difference: while the others came to visit me during the day and evening, Larisa expected to stay. She was on her first assignment—and I was it. For the KGB had sent Larisa to be my live-in lover.

Chapter Eleven

Russian Winter

The Kiev Express rolled south into the night. The four of us—Victor, Vladimir, Larisa and myself—chatted, then tried to get some sleep.

At 8 a.m. a steward brought some hot lemon tea and a half-hour later we pulled into Kiev's beautiful train station, adorned with marble walls and ornate ironwork. People rushed to and fro, carrying every possible kind of suitcase, basket and package.

We were met by a cheerful man named Boris. He and his aide, Vladimir, were our hosts for the next five days. They drove us to a large *dacha* on the outskirts of the city. Separate rooms awaited us. Our host asked what I wished to see in Kiev. I told him I was interested in architecture, historic churches and museums.

Following breakfast, an Intourist guide gave us a tour of the city. Kiev, she told us, is considered the "mother city" of Russia. Russian civilization evolved here in the ninth century, and it was from Kiev that Christianity is said to have spread in the tenth century. We toured historical and cultural sites by day; at night we dined at a local restaurant or in our *dacha*.

Our visit to the Kiev War Memorial was especially moving. Located atop a hill, it consists of an enormous statue of Mother Russia, waving a sword to rally her sons in defense of the motherland. Down the hill, below her, the dead lay buried. A loudspeaker plays solemn hymns. Inside the museum, two displays made a strong impression on me.

The first was the ID card of an eleven year-old boy killed in a Nazi concentration camp. His photo remains etched in my mind. The second was the Soviet death count from World War II. The Soviet Union lost twenty million people. America lost 350,000—one fiftieth as many. All I can remember from my history in high school and college was that the United States and Great Britain won the war, defeating the Nazis with "some help" from the Russians. Twenty million people dead. That's some help! Kiev was leveled, along with many other Soviet cities. Imagine if we in the United States had suffered the equivalent of two or three Pearl Harbors in every state.

On a lighter side, Boris took us ice-fishing, to musical variety shows, and ballets, always managing the best seats. One night Boris took us to a musical. I remarked to Boris how gorgeous I found the lead actress. Boris smiled. Next night, he announced I would have dinner with her.

I was surprised and tried to beg off, but Boris lead me outside and pushed me into the back of his Volga. Sitting next to me was a lovely, sophisticated woman named Ludmilla. My Russian was poor, but I introduced myself. Ludmilla smiled. And off we drove to a restaurant for dinner with Vladimir and Boris. I laughed all the way home. Poor Ludmilla thought I was some foreign dignitary and didn't know what to make of me. Yet she was very kind, and helped Boris make a foreigner feel welcome in Kiev.

I learned in Kiev to give up being so introspective and egocentric. From the first day I walked onto Soviet soil, I had been obsessed with my own problems. In Kiev I learned how millions of people suffered and died—and how the survivors went on with life. I finally felt grateful. I was safe and well-fed, and, as far as I knew, my family was the same. Life produces hard times for all, and we must learn to cope. The English poet, John Donne, said it best when he wrote, "No man is an island, entire of itself."

We returned from Kiev by train, met by Sasha at the station. He was happy to see me and we joked all the way home about our escapades in Kiev.

We arrived back at my *dacha* and Larisa made the mistake of referring to it as "our home." This ended our relationship. I had enough problems to deal with, and I already had a wife I loved. Larisa's charms didn't go unnoticed by a man who had been separated from his wife for over three months, but within an hour, I cornered Sasha for a private chat and asked that the KGB find someone else to give Larisa language lessons. I effectively condemned myself to a winter without sex, but at least I wouldn't have to listen to Larisa's incessant giggling, either.

The double-defection of Vitaly Yurchenko, the Soviet KGB officer, on August 2, 1985, complicated my life in two different ways. I have already commented on the problems he caused by allegedly fingering me as "Robert," a Soviet informer within the CIA. That was the cause for the FBI's interest in me, their surveillance, and my eventual flight. Several months later, his re-defection back to the Soviet Union on November 2, 1985, resulted in severe clampdowns on my freedom of movement.

In October and November of 1985, the Western press finally reported Yurchenko's defection of several months earlier. One morning in November, I was amazed to hear on VOA that Yurchenko had taken refuge in the Soviet embassy in Washington, claiming that he had not defected but had been kidnapped by CIA agents in Rome. He also denied any cooperation with the American government. I doubt that anyone in either the KGB or CIA believed him, but the Soviets were glad to take him back.

My situation worsened immediately after Yurchenko's re-defection. My team was determined never to let happen to them what had happened to the dim-witted CIA escort whom Yurchenko slipped away from. By December, 1985, a guard or team member accompanied me wherever I went. I couldn't take a walk outside the *dacha* perimeter without at least two guards, and when in Moscow, I was never beyond sight of my team members. I recall one night I went for dinner in Moscow to the Restaurant Peking with Victor and Vladimir. I excused myself to use the toilet, but found my two KGB colonels flanking me at the urinal within ten seconds of unzipping my trousers. No one was going to ruin their careers having a defector slip away during a trip to the john!

Christmas, 1985 was soon to arrive, destined to become the saddest Christmas of my life. Vladimir and Victor did their best to make it cheerful for me. They ordered a large Christmas tree with lights, and took me to an Eastern Orthodox church service. On Christmas day the whole team came by for a meal, and we exchanged presents. My favorite was from Sasha: two framed, enlarged photos of my wife and son. Unbeknownst to me, he had borrowed my wallet-sized photos, had them copied, enlarged and framed—all in a day. I was deeply touched by this gift. My eyes moistened. After the team left, I looked out from my garden room onto the beautiful snow-covered pine trees and prayed for all of my family to know that I was okay and thinking of them.

A week later was New Year's, a major Russian holiday. I knew that Victor, Vladimir and Sasha would want to be with their families, so I asked them not to stay with me that evening. I spent New Years Eve alone, listening to jazz and drinking champagne. I wandered down to the *dacha*'s guard shack to smoke cigars with them.

With January came endless snow. It marked the start of a very dark period of my life. Everything, it seemed, was either hopeless or in limbo. I spent countless hours at night in front of the fireplace, reading. By day, I went skiing. I allowed myself to become depressed. I drank too much too often, seeking relief and escape from my personal tragedy, only to wake up with a hangover—and the same problems.

Igor lectured me about my drinking. But he understood. "You need work. Something to occupy your mind. Don't become lazy," he would say.

I knew Igor was right, but it seemed like the date to call my wife in March would never arrive.

To break my depression, Sasha suggested I travel south with him in early February, to Soviet Georgia. It would be warmer, he said. I agreed in an instant.

Chapter Twelve

Moscow Station

No one outside the CIA and the KGB has known what my real assignment was to have been in Moscow, nor have any of the self-proclaimed intelligence experts ever come close to guessing it. I wasn't being sent to run spies, as intelligence pundits have written with such smug certainty.

Soon after I began work in the CIA's Soviet division, I had access to two types of files. The first was the weekly surveillance activity reports, detailing who had spotted which Soviet surveillance teams, where and when. The second were routine reports on non-sensitive, ongoing projects such as radiation measurements picked up by our station officers as they drove by various Soviet scientific institutes.

About this time, Mary was transferred from the CIA Language School to work as a secretary on the Soviet desk. She had completed the Denied Area Operations Course together with me, and her secretarial position gave her better understanding of the day-to-day operations in Moscow than I had.

By August I had completed my Russian studies at Georgetown University and I returned to the Soviet desk for a month of full-time work before Mary and I commenced the CIA Russian language course at the Arlington Chamber of Commerce building. About that time, Mary told me she was pregnant, and we asked for permission to take a week's leave together so that we could enjoy a short vacation before more language training—and parenthood.

My last few months in Washington in the spring of 1983 left me little time for myself or Mary, since I had full-time language training, files to read at the Soviet desk, my "cover" integration as a U.S. diplomat at the State Department and weekends at The Farm.

The press has written that I allegedly "rolled up" or exposed the CIA's human assets in Moscow, and that my alleged collusion with the KGB resulted in the arrest and execution of a Russian scientist and CIA informant named Adolf G. Tolkachev and other spies.

I want to reiterate what I have maintained for nine years: not only am I not responsible for the arrest or death of anyone, but the CIA's compartmentalization procedures ensured that I did not even have access to the information it is alleged that I passed to the Soviets.

Since I've cited these compartmentalization procedures in my defense, I will take this opportunity to explain them generally.

In Langley, when I was getting my training, everything was "by the book," and compartmentalization was the order of the day. I didn't know the names or identities of any agents. I only saw an occasional, encrypted codename, like "JKHarry." When a spy is recruited, his name goes into a black envelope that is dispatched to a safe in the basement. Anyone who needs to see the spy's name or identification must get the approval of the division chief and sign a ledger showing that he has had access to the information. I had no need to know the agents' names, and I never asked for nor was granted access.

The Soviet desk, of course operated under the same compartmentalized, "need-to-know" procedures. It was my job to read cable traffic from the Moscow station. Since I was busy all week with language and State Department training, I'd go in to Langley on the weekends and read the surveillance reports. Every officer at the Moscow station was required to turn in a weekly report listing all the times that he knew he was being watched by the KGB. The station even had a contest to see who could identify the most surveillance incidents each week. They had a list of known KGB license plate numbers, and at the end of each week, the Chief of Station would announce, "The prize goes to John Smith, who noted eleven surveillance contacts this week."

Station cables don't lay around for anyone to browse. They are locked in safes, and if you are not cleared for access to a set of files, you don't get the combination to that safe.

There was a general reading file in a safe behind the secretary's desk. I was required to read those files, and I had the combination for that safe. Each officer is also assigned his own desk and personal safe, and the specialized papers that I was supposed to read were put in my personal safe for me. I had no access to the safes of other officers who were working with the assets in the field. Access was strictly controlled. I did not have access to information on Moscow station's human assets.

It has been alleged that I revealed the names of CIA human assets in Moscow to the KGB. This is not true. I never knew the names of any agents in the first place so I couldn't possibly have exposed them.

According to a published interview with convicted spy Aldrich Ames, the advent of networked personal computers and shared computer databases has led to a gradual breakdown of the CIA's "compartmentalization" procedures. This breakdown permitted Ames to gain access to almost any information he wanted to sell to the Russians.

In the early 1980s, when I was trained, the PC had not yet arrived. The CIA maintained strict compartmentalization procedures. A person was given access to only that secret information for which he had a legitimate need to know. Yet it has been alleged that I, in preparation for Moscow Station, had access to detailed information about virtually all the technical and personal assets known to the CIA in Moscow. Not only is this allegation untrue, but it makes no sense at all.

Aldrich Ames worked in the Soviet division's counter-intelligence section, thus giving him access to the names of some Soviet agents before they were recruited and their names sealed. I use the word "some" since Ames did not spend his entire nine-year spying period in that section. I never worked in the counter-intelligence section, and, therefore, never had access to the names of potential agents before their recruitment.

I did see some agent communication plans while I worked on the Soviet desk. These plans are computer-generated and list the dates, times and sites for agent meetings for a year in advance.

The meeting sites are not listed by address, but by codes, and the agents are listed only by code name. The communication plan for a given meeting would read something like this: "Agent XYZ is scheduled to contact us at site Delta on May 1, 1994 at 4:00 p.m." The location of site "Delta" is kept in a safe in Moscow, since the Washington case officers have no need to know the location of the sites.

The information provided to the CIA officer in Moscow by the agent is not sent to the Soviet desk, but is sent directly to a special reports section at Langley. Therefore, those who sit at the Soviet desk never see the information that the agents produce. The special reports section does report back to the Soviet desk and to the CIA station in the embassy whether or not the information was useful.

These are the general procedures that the CIA uses to compartmentalize secret information. Only those with a legitimate "need to know" may gain access to a given piece of information.

This exchange of "You did it!" and "No, I didn't!" is what I have privately called "the pissing match," which no one will ever resolve for certain, even if the whole matter were to go to court. For that reason, I will not prolong the pissing match, but I will simply tell you what little I learned about CIA human agent operations in Moscow during my training in 1983. You, the reader, can judge whether or not I was capable of endangering U.S. national security by telling the KGB all I knew when I came here in September of 1985, as others have alleged.

I knew for certain that the CIA was dealing with human agents in Moscow in 1983. This came from reading cables to which I had access. I never knew their names.

It has been alleged that I revealed information that led to the death of several Russian agents, but the name of only one has been specifically laid at my doorstep: Adolf G. Tolkachev, a Russian military electronics expert who was arrested by the KGB in the summer of 1985, was tried, convicted and shot. The allegations linking me with Tolkachev's execution still bother me. Although I didn't arrive in Moscow until more than three months after his arrest, I was blamed for blowing his cover.

Writer David Wise questioned me about Tolkachev in 1987 when he was researching his biography of me. Wise quoted me as saying that Tolkachev "very well could be one of the assets I would have handled." In fact, my job was not to be running human assets. Wise took the Tolkachev ball and ran with it because I never told him my true mission.

It got to be a big joke among the KGB team guarding me to laugh and kid me about my "good work" every time an American diplomat somewhere in the world was arrested for espionage. They knew the CIA would use me as the whipping boy.

One day I asked Igor about Tolkachev. Igor refused to talk about him, dismissing Tolkachev as "just another American spy." Another time, at Yasenevo for dinner, I summoned up my courage to ask General Anatoly Tihanovitch, the KGB counter-intelligence chief, about the Tolkachev case. He studied me for a minute and said, "Yes, my officers have told me that you are concerned about the man and the press reports linking you to his execution."

He then confided in me the sad details which, until now, have been known only by a few people in the West. He said that Tolkachev was an electronics engineer working for the CIA. Tolkachev's specialty was Soviet radar, a type known as "look down, shoot down" radar. Before the Soviets had identified him, they knew they had a security leak in this area, because aircraft engagements in the Middle East had shown that the Western powers knew too much about Soviet radar.

General Tihanovitch did not tell me how the KGB unmasked Tolkachev. He implied that the KGB used him for counter-intelligence purposes for some time before his arrest. Intelligence services often do this in order to feed false information to the enemy and study how he was being handled. How long he had been cooperating with the KGB, I don't know, but if the CIA was meeting Tolkachev in 1983 and this was known to the KGB, Tolkachev's undoing could well have been Aldrich Ames.

After General Tihanovitch broke the ice with me about Tolkachev, Igor told me more about him. He told me that Tolkachev was a closet fascist. Until that time, I didn't know that the "A" in A. G. Tolkachev stood for "Adolf." I had never seen his first name in the press or anyplace else. Then my mind clicked. We had sent the book *Mein Kampf* to an agent in 1982 or 1983! Igor added that in 1985, after his arrest, Tolkachev stated during his interrogation that he believed in the "superior German race."

Igor told me that the KGB found two interesting things when they searched Tolkachev's apartment: scores of empty vodka bottles and 400,000 rubles in cash. In 1985, four-hundred thousand rubles was enough money to pay the annual salary of a KGB colonel for sixty-five years. Tolkachev was not motivated by altruism, ideology or revenge. Like Aldrich Ames, he was in it solely for the money.

For me, the saddest part was not Tolkachev's execution, but the fact that he had recruited his wife, a communications specialist, to hand him additional secret information to pass onto the CIA. I don't think the CIA ever knew that his wife was a source of his information. If she had been known to the CIA, standard operating procedures would have dictated that she also be given a code name. Since, to my knowledge, she had none, it is my belief that Tolkachev ran his wife without CIA knowledge. Nevertheless, she was arrested along with him, although I never learned whether she, too, was executed.

Fascist scientist—Adolf G. Tolkachev—lost his life, and possibly his wife, too, in the name of national security.

There wasn't much return for the huge cost in dollars, careers and lives spent on running Moscow Station.

Chapter Thirteen

Homeward Bound

My trip to Georgia was impending and Sasha, planning to accompany me, was excited. His grandfather came from there—"Just like Stalin," he said.

But just before our departure in mid-February, Sasha received bad news. His grandmother had taken ill and, afraid she might die, he chose to stay in Moscow with her. I would travel without my friend, accompanied again by Victor and Vladimir.

We flew to the Tbilisi on a cold, snowy day, and were welcomed by a Georgian KGB general called "Dabid" and his four guards. We were driven to a well-guarded *dacha* on the outskirts of the Georgian capital.

Only men were present when dinner was served, as was the custom in Georgia. Women served our meal. I began to suggest how nice it would be to have the women join us, but this was met with a frown from the General—and a stiff "don't ask" look from Victor. Later, one of our Georgian hosts summed up his philosophy about women this way: "They should be well cared for in order that they can wash your feet every day."

I was in Georgia for five days and divided my time between museums, dining out and a visit to Stalin's birthplace at Gori. I was struck by the generosity of Georgians. They love to entertain, and they are known for their long toasts and gracious hospitality.

I became ill with a virus while visiting the town of Sin-udali. My host made me drink six ounces of sha-sha, a strong Georgian vodka made from grapes. The drink knocked me out cold. But, as promised, I had no hangover the next morning and the virus was gone.

Then I fell into a terrible melancholy. It prompted me, as we drove back to Tblisi, to announce that I wanted to return home to the United States.

Victor got angry and a yelling match broke out in the car. He ordered the driver to go faster. Soon, we were traveling over 130 kilometers an hour through winding roads. The driver was frightened, but he knew better than to argue with a KGB colonel. I got so scared that I shut up. Victor quieted down, too, and we resumed a normal speed for the rest of our trip back to Tbilisi. Victor and I didn't speak that night. We flew back to Moscow the next day as if the incident hadn't happened.

By late winter, 1986, my anxiety worsened. What was happening to my wife and son? How were my parents handling all of this? What problems was the FBI making for my family? On one hand, I felt that I had to get home and help them through this horrible mess. But viewed objectively, I knew that my presence would only worsen our situation. I would probably be caught before I got within a mile of my family. I was in an emotional quagmire; damned if I do and damned if I don't.

Near the end of February, Igor told me that Generals Kryuchkov and Tihanovitch wanted to have dinner with me. He said that the Soviet leadership felt that Moscow was the only place I would ever see my family again, and they thought it was finally time to officially announce my presence in the Soviet Union. Igor told me that if I accepted this proposal, I should prepare a list of my needs and present it to the generals at dinner.

I considered this for several days. They were asking me to make a clean break with my past life in America and officially become the first CIA officer to defect to the Soviet Union.

Accepting their offer would make it possible for me to take control of my life and start designing my own future. Coming out would also enable me to negotiate directly with the American government about my case. But it would also make me appear guilty of having sold out the CIA's secrets, and this might make life harder for my family.

For the Soviets, my defection would be a tremendous propaganda coup. It would also be a major recruiting aid to the KGB, who would be able to say to prospective spies, "Look how well we treated Ed Howard when he defected."

I provisionally decided to accept their invitation to defect, subject to one condition: that I be able to phone my wife and discuss this with her. Igor approved the call, but said it should come after the discussion with the generals.

The dinner was held at the end of February in the guest *dacha* at Yasnevo where I had spent my first three weeks. This was an important business meeting, and it was conducted in a formal style. Everyone dressed in conservative suits. There were five persons sitting at the table: General Vladimir Aleksandrovitch Kryuchkov, head of the First Main Directorate of the KGB; General Anatoly Tihanovich Kiril, head of Soviet counterintelligence, Colonel Igor Anatolyivitch Batamirov, acting as translator, my friend, Sasha— and me.

Galinina, the cook, prepared a marvelous meal, consisting of salmon, caviar, sturgeon, cold meats, tongue, ham, and the main course, chicken. There was plenty of vodka, champagne, and Chivas Regal scotch, General Kryuchkov's preferred drink.

As the senior general, Kryuchkov formally proposed that I defect to the Soviet Union and join the Communist Party. He said that openly defecting was the only practical way to reunite my family. In return, I would be granted Soviet citizenship, and I would be guaranteed a good job, shelter, and a good life for my family.

I said I was comfortable with defecting, but not with joining the Communist Party. I politely declined that part of his offer, saying, "I'm not a political person. I'm an economist."

Kryuchkov saw through my charade, and told me that "no one can escape politics," and that I would see the day when I would have to choose one side to stand with. It was a lecture, albeit a kind one. (Although there is new leadership in Russia today, I still respect many of the "old school" types like Kryuchkov who could not understand the forces that were then building and which brought about the Russia of today.)

Kryuchkov didn't push party membership. He asked me what I would require if I were to make my life in the Soviet Union. I told him that I would need a resettlement package similar to what I would receive if I were leaving employment with one firm in the United States and joining another firm based abroad.

In the United States, I left behind a $95,000 house, my furniture, clothes and other personal possessions, a Jeep and an Oldsmobile, a good job and salary, my Social Security benefits and my health care plan. The KGB agreed to replace these things on a similar scale. (They did a good job; today I am comfortable.)

I was granted Soviet (now Russian) citizenship and assigned a furnished apartment in Moscow. It has two bedrooms, a bath, a kitchen, a dining room, a living room and a balcony. It is conveniently situated in a modern building in an old, relatively quiet part of Moscow, close to Arbat-skaya (Arbat Street), about one kilometer from the Kremlin. Our tenants' association employs a full-time door keeper, who provides security and keeps the entrance clean. That's the mark of a prestigious residence here. In the United States, it would be considered an unexceptional, middle-class apartment, although by Russian standards, it's very large and luxurious. After Boris Yeltsin came to power, Russian citizens were given the opportunity to privatize their residences at nominal cost. I did so in 1992, and now I own my apartment, responsible only for utilities and maintenance.

My relocation package included a sum of money to use to build a future home of my own, the use of a government-owned *dacha* in Zhukovka, an upscale, residential suburb about twenty minutes outside Moscow; a 1987 Volvo station wagon, annual plane tickets for my family and a moderate salary.

I was paid the salary during the five years it took for me to develop a private business and become self-sufficient. When I told the KGB in 1991 that I would move to Sweden to make my life and fortune, they told me, "If you leave, you can always come back and live in the *dacha*, but financially, you're on your own." I've been financially independent of the Russian government and the KGB since 1991.

I told the generals that I wanted to work in economics, with no connection with any intelligence service. I told them I would need econometric software for my computers and a subscription to D.R.I., an international economic database. General Vladimir Aleksandrovitch asked what D.R.I. was, and I told him. I explained that the CIA considered economic information to be the most important intelligence data of the future.

When I talked about D.R.I. and the software, Kryuchkov stopped and laughed. "I know about your economic work for the CIA. It's interesting," he said. But he made it clear that he thought military and political information was much more important.

I encountered that same mentality at Langley when I left in 1983. Six years after our dinner, General Kryuchkov had made a 180 degree turn in his opinions, and made a public statement stating that the KGB's first priority would be economic intelligence.

Before I ended my speech, I added a caveat. Before anything was announced, I wished to consult my wife. Kryuchkov agreed, but he warned me about expecting too much, since, he said, she was still under the thumb of the FBI.

I told Kryuchkov that it had been six months since I left the United States, and that the FBI should have forgotten about her by now.

"No, that's not true, Ed," he whispered. "One of our officers made a drive by your home in Santa Fe last month and found a car parked near your house with two sleeping FBI officers inside."

I wondered if this was true, or fabricated to frighten me. Later, my wife would tell me that the FBI kept surveillance on her for only a couple of months and that during the Christmas season of 1985 they resumed surveillance, believing that a lonely, emotional Ed Howard would return home to his family. They were half right: I had dearly wanted to return.

The generals left in their respective staff cars and Igor, Sasha and I stayed behind at the *dacha* to polished off the Chivas Regal. We discussed the phone call to my wife.

A few weeks later, I sat waiting in the servant's quarters of my *dacha* for the call to be put through. The call was being placed to my house in Santa Fe, so we assumed the FBI would be listening. The Soviets had gone to great lengths to ensure that they could not trace the call.

Vladimir told me that the call was first routed to another socialist country, then overland to a Western country. From there it was beamed to a satellite then down into the U.S. telephone system. It sounded like something out of *Star Wars.*

The phone rang. Mary answered. I could hardly hear her voice through all the static. We talked for seven or eight minutes. Mary asked how I was and where I was—a question, it seemed, straight out of an FBI script. I told her I was in a safe place, and asked if she and Lee could come join me.

Mary said no, but that they really wanted me to come home. This, too, sounded like the FBI talking. But I felt the emotion in her voice and knew of her care for me, despite the FBI's pressure on her. Again and again I asked if she and Lee would be willing to join me in "a safe place where we could live in peace," but I always got the same response: "Come home and let's talk." After seven or eight frustrating minutes, I couldn't take any more of the terrible connection or of not being able to talk to my wife without both the FBI and KGB listening. I said good-bye to Mary, told her I loved her, and that I would do what I could about our future.

Igor and Sasha arrived at the *dacha* an hour after the call. They found me severely depressed. Although they had probably listened in at headquarters, I recounted the conversation for them.

"I must get to Mary soon," I added, "and find out the truth from her personally."

"That's almost impossible without having her come here," Igor responded. "Become open and you can see her here."

"No. I must go to her. I want you to keep your promise to let me go if I choose. I appreciate all your help until now, but now I'm calling the shots, and I must leave soon."

"But what about your agreement to defect?" asked Igor.

"That's canceled because of this phone call. She wants me home. I'll get to her and my son and find a neutral place somewhere to live."

Igor's mood darkened and he prepared to leave. "Very well, Ivan Ivanovitch. I'll report your wishes to the management and see what they have to say."

Igor and Sasha drove off, and I felt relieved but scared by the implications of my choice. At last I would get to see my family. But what if I was caught along the way? It was time to develop a plan.

For weeks, I studied world maps and maps of the United States, analyzing how I would approach my family and where I could take them.

In the days following my decision to leave, Victor, Vladimir and Sasha fell into a somber mood. They didn't comment on my decision and didn't want to discuss any aspects of it. Igor, who usually dropped by every two or three days, seemed to be avoiding me.

Towards the end of March I grew frustrated by their lack of action on my decision to leave. My questions about what preparations were being made or when I could leave were met with a polite reply that boiled down to, "all in good time."

I pondered what I could do to speed up the process. I couldn't phone the generals because I was never given their numbers. Victor, Vladimir and Sasha were my buffers and baby-sitters, with no power to make decisions.

My comfortable *dacha* had become a gilded cage—and no one likes to be held against their will.

I tried to think what I could do to force them to let me go. I came up with only two options: Call the U.S. embassy or stage a protest strike. Calling the U.S. embassy for help would only land me in the waiting arms of the FBI. So I chose the "hippie activist" approach, a sit-down strike. But where? I couldn't sit down in Kryuchkov's office. All I had was my *dacha*.

The answer came to me on snowy evening late March: "Go up on the roof and don't come down until they agree to talk seriously." I had a one-story *dacha* with an inclined roof that would be safe to sit on—as long as I didn't fall asleep.

I packed a blanket, a bottle of red wine, apples and oranges and my Swiss Army knife into a large bag. I put on my Finnish winter jacket and left my *dacha* via the kitchen door, avoiding Vladimir, who was watching television at the time. It was 6 p.m.

Outside, I used a metal ladder to climb onto the roof, and made my way to the center. Almost immediately, one of my four uniformed guards noticed me.

"Ivan, what are you doing up there?" he asked in Russian.

"What does it look like?" I replied. "I have a blanket and food, and I will be up here for a long time."

The guard immediately called his companions and one went to tell Vladimir what was happening. Vladimir came outside, stared up in amazement and shouted, "Ed, you'll get cold up there. Come down and we'll talk."

"Don't worry, Vladimir," I called down. "I'm not going to jump, but I plan to stay up here until you guys give me a decent response to my plans to leave. I have my coat, a blanket and a bottle of good Georgian wine to keep me warm. We've been talking for weeks, but nothing is happening."

The evening wore on. Vladimir phoned Sasha, and they both tried in vain to talk me down. Next, Igor showed up, and his jaw dropped open in amazement when he saw me on the roof.

At about nine, my next-door neighbor and his entourage of guards and aides showed up at our mutual fence to take in the spectacle. I didn't know him by name at the time, but I knew that he was a silver-haired man who was General Secretary of the Communist Party for Moscow. Months later, I learned his name: Boris Nikolaivitch Yeltsin, now President of Russia. I imagine I made quite an impression on him!

Past ten, it grew very cold, and with Sasha, Igor and Vladimir promising to discuss my problem seriously, I came down. By Western standards, it wasn't much of a protest, but to my Soviet caretaker team it was astonishing, because they were not used to putting up with such anti-social behavior among their own citizens.

On the ground, Igor hugged me. We went inside, drank hot tea—and Igor promised me to consult with management about my problem the next day. I went to bed feeling like a fool, and wondering whether any good would come of my college stunt.

The next day was Victor's turn to baby-sit me, and he shook his head when he saw me. "You really stirred up the hornet's nest last night, my friend. Your neighbor, Boris Yeltsin, who is a member of the *Politburo*, called General Chebrikov and asked what was going on here. Chebrikov called for

Kryuchkov, who had to explain the whole thing. It's Kryuchkov that I'm worried about. You should do every-thing possible to keep him as your friend."

The next afternoon, Vladimir dropped by unexpectedly. "I just had a conference with General Kryuchkov. He asked me if they really do such crazy things in America. He shook his head in disbelief when I told him that when I was working in America, the college students would march, seize offices and hold sit-down strikes. He has never lived in the West, so this behavior is all new to him."

I was happy to hear this. He didn't think I was crazy, just a typical, anti-authoritarian American. "Tell the generals that I apologize for my behavior. I'm homesick and I just want to get to see my family."

"We all know that. The General is assigning another man to the team here. His name is Alex Mikhailavitch Kazlov, and he spent two years in a South African prison before they traded him back to us. He worked many years as an undercover officer and knows how difficult that life can be. Since you have chosen to leave, this man will provide you with the training you will need to escape and evade your enemies. He will also tell you how to survive in prison if you get caught. And you probably will," Vladimir added. "He's coming here tomorrow."

My spirits soared. I ignored Vladimir's prognosis that I would probably end up in prison, and focused on getting out of my golden cage. I also secretly smiled, knowing that my childish roof prank had driven them to action.

Alex arrived the next day and I took an instant liking to him. He was about fifty years old and spoke excellent English and German. He had twenty years' experience working as an intelligence officer. He walked in constant pain from the beatings he received in his two years in a South African prison. Nevertheless he had a lust for life and a good sense of humor.

"If you're foolish enough to go through with your plans, I must prepare you physically and mentally," he told me. "We will exercise twice a day and discuss tradecraft: how to handle border crossings, police questioning, documents, life-style when you are hiding, and emergency escape plans.

"Another thing," he added. "I will not tolerate any more of this petty brooding about your family. You won't have time for that. You're going to work like a dog for the six weeks that I have to prepare you, and if you're going to stand even a ten percent chance of success, you must be very strong emotionally as well as physically. The house bar is now closed, except for an occasional beer at dinner—and then, only if I think you earned it."

Now I knew that the KGB was serious about letting me go back.

Every day before breakfast, Alex instructed me to jog at least five kilometers and do exercises with him. Later, as he fed me information about my new identity, he peppered me with questions as we jogged, grilling me about who I was, when I was born, why I had Danish border stamps in my passport—and a hundred other vital details.

Alex was a worldly man who had lived life on the streets and had an answer for everything. If, for instance, I needed to explain a stamp in my false passport that showed I had crossed into Denmark from Sweden at Malmo, Alex advised the following: "All the Swedish men go whoring in Denmark, then come back drunk on the boat the next day, and Customs doesn't even want to smell them. They stamp their passports without even looking and wave them through."

He gave me many other practical tips, such as flying on Malev, the Hungarian airline, whose computers were not yet linked to Western airline reservation computers. The CIA, I recalled from my training at Langley, regularly tapped the airline computers to track travelers in whom they took an interest.

Alex also taught me to stash spare documents and cash in a safe place near my residence. "Always approach your house as if someone was waiting to catch you. Make sure you detect them before they see you. If you do, get the documents and money you need from your pre-arranged hiding place and take the quickest and most discreet way out of town, following your pre-arranged evacuation plan."

I grew to enjoy Alex's company. In the evenings, after the day's training was done, we would sit by the fireplace and chat. He told me he once had a wife and children, and how hard it was to keep up contact with them while he was in the West. After his imprisonment, his wife gave up on him and went with another man. When he returned from South Africa, he only had his daughter. He found another woman, though his first wife wanted to come back to him. "Remember, Ed, we have a saying, 'A man can have many wives, but his children are always his children.' " That was not much comfort to me at the time, because I didn't want to think that my wife or son would give up on me. I wanted to be reunited with both of them.

In early May Igor stopped by to check my progress. He told me that General Yuri Drozdov, a former KGB resident in America, and now head of the program which trained and ran the KGB's undercover officers, was personally supervising the preparation of the documents I would soon receive.

A few days later, Igor brought me a photocopy of the U.S. passport I was to use in the West. It bore the name Scott Alan Roth, and stated that I had been born in Pennsylvania on December 12, 1949—two years earlier than my actual birth date. Igor assured me that it was a valid U.S. passport, but would not explain where or how they obtained it.

I set about memorizing every detail of my new passport and the answers to every question I might be asked about it, such as the visas and border stamped upon its pages. I familiarized myself with the other fake identity documents: My driver's license, library card and immunization record.

I also had to have a good legend (cover story) for everything I planned to do and every place I planned to be. I spent countless hours memorizing my new legend with the help of my team members, who posed as customs officers, policemen and border guards to help me prepare for every possible contingency.

Late in May, Sasha announced that the time to depart was nearing. Igor announced that on the last Friday in May, General Anatoly Tihanovitch would come for dinner and personally give me all the details.

"What about Kryuchkov?" I asked.

Igor said he was too busy, but I knew that he was disappointed by my wish to leave.

General Tihanovitch first showed me my Soviet diplomatic passport. It was issued on May 28, 1986. I would use it for crossing into Austria, where Soviet diplomats needed no visas.

Then he gave me the Scott Alan Roth passport for my further travel. In essence, the Soviets would get me into Austria and then I was on my own. They gave me some cash for travel and living expenses and a way I could contact them if I needed assistance.

"The most important thing we can give you, Ivan"—Anatoly always referred to me as Ivan—"is this bit of information: We know your wife is under the thumb of the FBI. We have told you this, but you do not believe us. You prefer to let your big heart dictate to your mind. When you reach the United States, we urge you to make contact with a friend of ours in the U.S. He can prove to you that she is under their control and is obliged to turn you in to the FBI should you approach her."

The General then gave me verbal instructions about how to contact the "friend." He did not allow me to make any notes, except to write a telephone number in reverse order on a piece of paper that would dissolve instantly if I swallowed it. I thanked the General and told him I valued his advice and would meet with the friend before meeting my wife.

"It is a risk for us also," he said, "but General Kryuchkov wants you to win. We all want you to win. We trust you and believe that you will do everything to protect everyone here, should things not go well for you."

I swore to him and to myself that the FBI would never get that phone number or any details of who or where the "friend" was, in the event that I was caught. I will honor that promise forever.

The next question I had for General Anatoly was my departure date.

"Tomorrow," he said. "You will fly in our Chairman's private plane to Bratislava, Czechoslovakia. Then you will be driven across the border to Vienna about lunch time."

I swallowed hard. All the waiting, all the planning and training, and it was going to happen tomorrow!

The team, General Anatoly and I all had a quiet dinner together. The General wished me luck in a warm, personal toast and I thanked them all for their help and patience. Then as a souvenir, I gave the General my TWA "Getaway" credit card for their museum. He laughed and hugged me.

The General announced that the bar was closed for the evening and said good-bye, leaving me with Sasha, Alex and Vladimir. They helped me pack, discarding anything that came from the U.S.S.R., including plastic combs, pens and even the laundry stickers on my clothes, which would identify me as having lived in a *Politburo dacha*. I tossed and turned all night.

I was on my way—covertly—to the United States. Would I end up in the arms of my wife—or the FBI?

Chapter Fourteen

Illegal Entry

Saturday, June 1, 1986. I had been away for eight months. The big day arrived to start my journey home. It began with Vladimir and Alex thoroughly inspecting my possessions— yet again—for any trace of Soviet-made items. They gave me two worn, American-made suitcases.

We had a final breakfast together, then Alex said good-bye and wished me luck. Vladimir, Igor and I were driven to Vnukovo, Moscow's southern airport, and joined by Viktor and Alexander, a KGB officer from Vienna. A gleaming Tupolov 154 awaited us on the tarmac. It was the private jet of General Viktor Chebrikov, Chairman of the KGB. The plane had a capacity for 125 passengers, so there was plenty of room for our small party!

I said good-bye to Igor, thanked him for all he had done —and then we were off—a two-and-a-half-hour flight to Czechoslovakia. We talked quietly; I read. I was nervous.

We landed at Bratislava airport on the Czech-Austrian border. Vladimir remained in the plane with me while Viktor and Alexander dealt with Customs and Immigration, smoothing my entry. They returned and we exchanged hugs.

I was whisked off the plane and into a Soviet diplomatic car without slowing for a moment. Alexander sat in back with me; two KGB officers sat up front. We reached the border in 15 minutes, across the Danube River to Austria. Passport Control held us for only a minute and we were through. I had cleared my first hurdle. I was back in the West.

It was only a thirty-minute drive from the Danube to Vienna, but the two Vienna-based KGB agents spent an hour-and-a-half ensuring we were not being followed. We drove throughout the entire city, frequently changing speed and direction. At one point we were passed by a light-colored German car and the passenger waved to our front-seat passenger. This was clearly some sort of counter-surveillance signal process -- just like the CIA training exercises I'd participated in five years before. We were graded on a 0-7 scale for our performance. This time, there were only two grades: "pass," for avoiding arrest, or "fail," which would mean spending the rest of my life in prison.

Finally, the front passenger looked back at Alexander and said *"Vseo-v-poryadke"* (Everything is in order). We drove to a taxi stand and I got out. They handed me my luggage and my fake U.S. identity documents.

I got into a taxi and asked to be taken to the Hotel President, which I had seen in a travel guide. It was mid-afternoon in Vienna, and I could relax until Monday. I went to the carnival, enjoyed the sausages and beer, walked through parks, took a sauna near my hotel and watched English-language programs in my room. It felt strange, exhilarating not to have a guard nearby or a member of my team watching my movements.

On Monday, June 3, I visited a bank to rent a safe deposit box for cash and some documents. Next I went to a travel agency and booked a one-way ticket for Calgary, in Alberta, Canada, north of Montana. I figured the best way to enter the United States would be from the west; that they wouldn't expect me from that direction.

That night I flew to Amsterdam and checked into an airport hotel. Next day, my flight to Canada was made more pleasant by a free upgrade.

Canadian customs is staffed chiefly by women, and I've always felt women have better intuition than men. The female immigration officer asked me what I was planning to do in Canada. I answered that I was meeting my wife and that we intended to visit the Exposition in Vancouver. Then she asked why I didn't have a round trip ticket back to Europe or to the U.S.A. I told her I was going to buy one later, when my plans were firm. With hindsight, the one-way ticket was a mistake. Now I always buy round-trip excursion tickets, even if I have to throw the unused, return ticket away. She asked me to take a seat, while other passengers cruised past me. That's when my adrenalin kicked in. A dark-haired female officer took me into a room with a computer. She punched in my passport data.

"Jesus," I thought. "I hope they really did give me a good passport in Moscow." Nothing bad appeared on the computer, so she asked if I had ever been incarcerated for a felony and how much money or credit cards I possessed.

"I've never even visited a prison," I said. "And I have about three thousand dollars in cash."

"Do you know if your wife is waiting for you here to drive you to the Exposition in Vancouver?" she asked.

"She better be, after I've flown all this way!"

"Okay. Get your bags and have a good time. Don't bother to take them through the inspection."

I cleared the second hurdle and heaved a sigh of relief in the back of a taxi. At a residential hotel, I booked an efficiency apartment for the month and rested through the day to beat jet lag the rest of the day.

Next morning, I booked a flight to Salt Lake City, departing the following day. To protect the KGB's "friend," who I would soon meet, I can only say that, after Salt Lake City, I visited the eastern half of the United States. I can also say that my contact was not Aldrich Ames. I never knew my contact's name, and I ate the piece of paper with his phone number on it after I dialed it.

Again, I had a scare at Immigration. When you fly to the U.S.A. from Canada, you must clear U.S. Immigration before you board. I was not expecting this. I cleared the ticket counter and walked down the ramp to board the aircraft. I was greeted by the Stars and Stripes and a U.S. Immigration Officer.

"Got any identification?" he asked.

"Sure do." I handed him my Scott Alan Roth passport.

He studied it for a long time. "This looks funny."

"Why?" I asked.

"The printing of the middle name is darker than the first and last names."

I recalled the three rules of interrogation taught me by the CIA: One, deny everything. Two, admit nothing. Three, make counter-allegations.

"If that's a bad passport," I said, "I want my $35 back!"

"No . . . I guess its okay," he said. "Have a nice flight."

But this was a clever old bird, and I think he sensed my relief. I took just three steps away when he asked, "by the way, Mr. Roth, where were you born?"

Alamogordo, my true birthplace, was at the tip of my tongue. Then Alex's covert operations training screamed in my ears, *"Tee durak! Padumai!"* (Think, you idiot!).

"Pennsylvania," I said. "And where were you born?"

"Minot, North Dakota." He smiled.

"Why not Minot?" I laughed and walked onto the plane, ready for a well-earned nervous breakdown.

Chapter Fifteen

Desperation and Danger

I breathed another sigh of relief when my plane touched down in Salt Lake City. I had cleared my fourth major hurdle.

Then I traveled to a city in the eastern part of the United States and checked into a hotel near the airport. Next morning, Friday, I took a short bus ride, found a pay phone and called the number provided me by the KGB.

A male voice answered. I asked for a certain name. I was told I had dialed the wrong number. The man then said that my call was the second time someone had mistakenly dialed his number that day. That was the coded answer I was hoping to hear. The translation: "Meet me at the pre-designated park in two hours. Arrive dressed for jogging, and look for a male jogger dressed in the outfit which was described to you in Moscow."

I hurried back to my hotel and changed into jogging clothes. I didn't want to be late for the meeting, so I took a taxi to the park. A hundred questions raced though my mind. What kind of man was I meeting? What if he was under suspicion by the FBI and being followed? Or if he'd already been burned by the FBI and was working for them?

I arrived early and killed time doing warm-up stretches. Precisely, at the designated hour, my contact appeared. I approached with the recognition signal: I asked him a specific question about the park. He responded with the correct counter-sign and suggested we take a short jog together.

I was expecting someone fit and trim, like a KGB or FBI operations officer. This man—obviously not a Russian— looked like a mail-room clerk.

We jogged together for ten minutes. Then he motioned me to take a break and we sat upon a bench, set back among trees and bushes. He pulled a dossier of papers out of his jacket and handed it to me. These were classified documents from the U.S. Department of Justice and the FBI. I read through them quickly. The man made no comment and showed no emotion while I read.

I was in shock by the time I finished reading, about five minutes later.

These documents revealed to me that Mary had agreed to report to the FBI if she ever heard from me or saw me. It revealed that her phones were still tapped; that even when she had traveled to Hawaii on a vacation, she had checked in with the local FBI office; that she was under surveillance while in Hawaii.

The dossier expressed the government's confidence in my wife as an informant, and the Department of Justice felt that if I did contact her, she would tell them immediately. The report stated that my wife no longer wished to have com- munication with me, and implied that she was on the FBI's side.

It was a terrible, crushing disappointment for me. I felt real anger toward her for a short time. But after some reflection, I thought, "Why am I being so self-centered about all of this? What kinds of pressure and manipulation must she be going through every day as they interrogate her?"

I had been out of the United States and safe in a *Politburo dacha* full of food and servants. Mary, who had helped me escape, had to face a room full of angry FBI agents. Fortu- nately, I had not yet been charged with any crime before my escape, so Mary could not be charged as an accomplice.

But the FBI was laying a heavy guilt trip on her, and her family was pressuring her to disown me and cooperate with the FBI. Mary had to do what was best for herself and Lee.

I handed the documents back to my KGB contact. "Thanks," I said. "Do whatever you need to do to cover yourself."

"Good luck to you," he replied. "Forget everything you know about me."

I promised him that I would, and we parted, jogging off in different directions. He jogged over a hill and I never saw him again.

Someone might ask, "What if the man in the jogging suit was not an American government official, but an undercover KGB officer whose goal it was to scare me back to Moscow?"

It would be a perfect KGB operation. Let Joe Schmoe, the KGB undercover agent, show Howard some phony documents and he'll come running back. I don't think that was the case, but it shows the kind of world, of smoke and mirrors, I live in. Only a couple of men in downtown Moscow know the identity of the man I met. And they're not talking.

I was scared and confused. I felt like vomiting. Back at the hotel, I tried deep-breathing exercises to calm myself.

The FBI couldn't get their hands on me, so they'd gone after my wife. They threatened and interrogated her for three weeks after I left Santa Fe. At first she wouldn't tell them anything, but after day after day of intensive interrogation, she finally broke down and cooperated.

Mary told the FBI that she did not have any knowledge of my ever passing secret information to a foreign power, but did admit that it "could have been possible" during the few short times we were separated in Switzerland or Austria.

Once the FBI had coaxed the "possibility" factor out of Mary, they convinced her that she could face a jail term if she was ever caught in contact with me or harboring me. They threatened her with charges of harboring a fugitive if she didn't cooperate with them. They knew they couldn't prosecute her for obstruction of justice or aiding a fugitive, since her role in my escape was performed before any charges were filed against me.

Today I look upon my wife with great pride and deep love. In that difficult situation, she found a way to both honor her wedding vow to protect her husband, while still honoring her duty as an American citizen to cooperate with the authorities. During our years of separation since Santa Fe, she has lived in the United States, but she visits me regularly. Under trying circumstances, Mary has done an excellent job raising our son, and she has always been kind and fair with me. Our futures may not be together but she will always occupy the most special place in my heart.

I still wanted desperately to go see her and talk to her, and assure her I had done nothing wrong. Emotionally, that was all I could think about.

But I knew that attempting to visit Mary was now out of the question. Contact with me would only subject her to further harassment from the FBI; worse, they might try to prosecute her. Also, she was surrounded by friends and relatives who might think it best to protect her by calling the FBI if I were sighted.

My decision to abort an attempt to visit Mary was also influenced by the television news. I saw Ronald Pelton, the former NSA employee, sentenced to life in prison for espionage by a federal judge. He was practically in tears, and I swore I would never let that happen to me.

My mentor, General Kryuchkov, had been right. The only way that I would ever see my family again was to return to Moscow, defect, and invite them to openly visit me. It was time to put away the fantasies of whisking them out of the

United States and starting a new life in Argentina or Switzerland. The FBI would target my wife and son and track them until they found us. The life of a fugitive family was not what I wanted for Mary and Lee.

It was time for me to switch to "Plan B"—return to Moscow, if they'd take me back. After all I'd put my KGB friends through, I wondered if they really wanted to see me again. But I had little choice. That tortuous night, I began planning my return to the Soviet Union.

After only three days in the United States—hiding in hotel rooms, scurrying out at night to 7-11s for food and newspapers—I left. I flew back to Salt Lake City and found my way across the border into Canada.

I wasted no time clearing out my apartment in Calgary and booking a flight for Amsterdam. At the Amsterdam Marriott, I cut myself shaving and went to the hotel store for a Band-aid. It was just my luck that the *International Herald Tribune* was carrying my photo and an article about me on page three. I rushed to my room and booked a flight to Vienna.

I arrived in the Austrian capital the next day and made plans for a one-week stay at a Budapest health spa. I cleaned out the safe-deposit box I had rented ten days before, and I flew to Budapest.

Americans could obtain visas for visiting Hungary when they arrived at the airport. I told the Immigration officer I would be visiting Budapest for ten days. A travel agent in Vienna had helped me choose the perfect destination: the Margaret Hid Hotel, situated on an island in the Danube River. I was exhausted after my ten-day ordeal and needed a place to rest and think over my plans. The hotel had warm springs, saunas, good Hungarian food and a pleasant park.

I had often heard that Budapest was the "Paris of the East," and I concurred with this. Hungary certainly was not as socialist as Moscow. It had many fine restaurants and shops, and a pleasant climate. I began to consider Budapest as a possible home for me and my family.

On my first day in Budapest, I walked into the Soviet consulate and asked to see the embassy's security officer. A tall, middle-aged consular officer told me there was none, but invited me into a room to tell him about my problem. I showed him my U.S. passport and said that my real name was Edward Lee Howard, not Scott Alan Roth.

"Where did you get this passport?" he asked.

"Your people in Moscow gave it to me," I told him in Russian.

"Ah, so you speak Russian. Where did you learn it?"

"In Moscow. Please send a cable to Vladimir Aleksandrovitch and Anatoly Tihanovitch of the First Main Directorate." I said in Russian.

His jaw dropped. At first he may have thought I was some crank off the street. But when I rattled off the first names and patronymics of his KGB bosses, he knew I was serious.

"What would you have me tell these people?" he said, still trying to test me.

"I'll write the cable, but you must send it to the immediate attention of Victor Mikhailovitch and you'll get a fast response."

"Victor Mikhailovitch? You don't mean . . .," he stammered.

"Yes," I said. " Victor Mikhailovitch Chebrikov, the Chairman of the KGB."

"And just how do you know him?" he asked with a slightly dazed expression on his face.

"He was my dinner guest at a *dacha* in Veshki," I said. "Now if you'll just give me a couple of pieces of paper and a pen, I'll write a message."

This poor fellow had never had such a walk-in in all his career. He gave me pen and paper and I drafted a two-page cable to Moscow, describing my situation and requesting that Igor and Victor be sent to Budapest to confer with me.

The consular officer took note of where I was staying and said he would be in touch within a couple of days. It must be part of their training, I thought. That was the same line they gave me in Helsinki!

Next day, I found myself being followed around the park by a young man in a polo shirt and blue jeans. "Christ!" I thought. "The FBI wants me in the West and now the Hungarians are tailing me!"

After two days and no call from the Soviet consulate, I worried that my old friends no longer wanted me. I took a taxi to the consulate and the driver told me in German that General Secretary Mikhail Gorbachev was scheduled to visit Budapest that day. "Damn," I thought. "Embassy security will be so heavy I won't get within a hundred yards of the place."

But Gorbachev was not staying at the embassy. I was able to walk into the consulate, and I walked to a window where they take visa applications. Suddenly, a door opened in front of me. A man stepped out and we came face-to-face. He looked like Victor from Moscow. Our eyes met and we both panicked at each other's sight! He darted back into his office and I out the consulate door.

I stood there for ten seconds, wondering if I were going nuts. Then Victor dashed outside and pulled me into his office. Igor was there, standing at the desk, reading the hand-written cable I left for them two days before. He smiled and gave me a big hug. "How are you, Ed?"

"Boy, am I glad to see you two again!"

"The same for us," said Igor. "We were going to wait until tonight to contact you, because our General Secretary is in town today. He will leave tonight. But we are glad to see you now. Sit down and tell us all that has happened since Vienna."

I later learned that both the CIA and KGB "stand down" (discontinue) all foreign operational activities when a senior government official is in their area. This is done to avoid any chance of scandal for the official should something go wrong while they are in town. This is why Igor planned to wait until Gorbachev left Budapest before contacting me at my hotel.

I spent over an hour with my friends, recounting the events since I had left Vienna. "I know now that you were right," I said. "The only way I'll get to see my family again is with your help. I will defect and go public if Moscow will let me return."

"General Kryuchkov was very concerned for you and wanted us to learn what has happened and what your plans are for the future," said Igor. "You know we have no legal obligation to you, but we feel that we have a moral obligation to help you. I think everything will be all right, but I have to make my report to Moscow and wait for their directions."

"In either case, give them my best regards," I said. Then I couldn't resist asking, "Are you sure that was a good U.S. passport you gave me? They gave me hell about it going into the United States from Canada."

Igor examined the passport. "It's good, but even good things are not always perfect."

"I know, and I'm the perfect example," I joked.

We agreed to meet the next day for lunch at Igor's embassy apartment.

I explored Budapest, taking the sights and enjoying the warm mineral baths at the hotel. Finally, Igor announced that my Soviet diplomatic passport had arrived and that we had tickets on Aeroflot to Moscow the next day. He said my new *dacha* awaited me. I was elated.

I wanted only rest, peace and quiet. I knew what I had to do to see my family again. Yes, it would be very upsetting to my friends and family back home—and it would end all hope for a reconciliation with my country. But I had to make the only choice left to me. I would officially defect to the Soviet Union.

Chapter Sixteen

Safe House

I arrived back in Moscow the last week of June. My new *dacha*, a half-hour drive from the city-center, was in the small village of Zhukovka.

My new brick home was built in the *pri-baltiskaya* (Baltic Scandinavian) style. It is solid and spacious, if not stylish, possessing a huge living-dining room, two bedrooms, bathroom, study, kitchen and a covered patio. I was its first and only occupant, and it has been my permanent home since the summer of 1986.

The 5,000-square-foot compound includes a two-car garage, a two-room caretaker's house, and gardens in front and back. A small guardhouse is manned twenty-four hours a day by KGB guards who monitor a perimeter-wide, infrared alarm system.

Former President Richard Nixon visited Moscow that summer, so the announcement of my defection was delayed so as not to embarrass him. Still unofficial, I was confined to my *dacha*.

But once Nixon departed, I was permitted to walk around the village, visit the small shops, and jog in the woods with members of my team.

I have grown accustomed to my *dacha* like a man comes to love a faithful, ugly dog. Vasily Vasilovitch, the caretaker, and most of the guards have become my friends. Sometimes they watch television or a rented video with me. My KGB guards, unlike me, are great fans of Arnold Schwarzenegger.

In the summer I enjoy barbecuing on my patio; in the fall, I hunt for big juicy white mushrooms that abound in the wild. Come winter, I ski cross-country.

On August 7, 1986, the government newspaper, *Izvestia*, announced that the Soviet Union had granted me political asylum with the right to live and work in the U.S.S.R. Today, since all former Soviet citizens living in Russia are also citizens of Russia, I am a Russian citizen. I work here, pay taxes here and vote here like any other Russian citizen.

I never renounced my US citizenship. I still love my country. Under the Yeltsin constitution, it is legal for a Russian to hold dual citizenship, so my American citizenship poses no legal problem for me here. My U.S. passport has expired. When I travel, I use my Russian passport.

Igor had agreed that I could phone my wife and parents before my defection was announced. I knew they would be besieged by the media, so I wanted give them advance warning. So on August 5, I called Mary, who by then had moved from Santa Fe to live with her parents in Minnesota. I told her where I was, explained my situation and invited her and Lee to come visit.

Mary's reception to my call was cool. She told me not to worry about her and Lee, and that I should now concentrate on my own life. She said she didn't think it would be possible for her to visit Moscow, nor did she want to. She said I had made my choice to live in Moscow, but that she and my son would always prefer to live in the United States. I was deeply disappointed by the call. Again, I detected FBI influence.

Vladimir brought me a tape of the call. "There's lots of emotion in her voice, Ed," he said. "She still loves you."

I prayed that he was right, because I still loved my wife deeply and hoped that, in time, she would agree at least to visit me.

My call to my parents was more warmly received. After ten months of not knowing where or how I was, my mother and father were glad to hear from me.

I told them where I was.

"Are you treated well there?" asked my mother.

I told her that I was being treated very well.

"Good," my mother said. "Then stay there for now, because they'd just love to get their hands on you here."

Like mothers everywhere, my own ultimately was concerned only for my safety and happiness.

I, in turned, worried about her and my father, who worked for Texas Instruments, a defense contractor. Following the announcement of my defection, the Dallas press discussed whether my father should be permitted to continue to keep his job at Texas Instruments. Fortunately, good sense prevailed.

Following the announcement of my defection, the U.S. government told the Soviets they wanted to talk to me. I refused in writing to see them. The U.S. government then had the gall to ask the Soviets to turn me over to them.

"What did you tell them, Igor?" I asked.

"We told them to fuck off," said Igor.

It was one of the few times I heard cultured Igor swear. I nearly died laughing!

This exchange was funny, but it underscores the way the U.S. government does business abroad. If I had been granted political asylum in a small, non-nuclear country, the U.S. government would have bullied them to give me up. During the next few years, I witnessed this firsthand in Hungary and Sweden. Only the Soviet Union, a nuclear superpower, could make such a statement to the U.S. government and walk away without fear of reprisal.

I was depressed by my wife's position, so Igor suggested that Sasha take me on a visit to Tallinn in Estonia in mid-August for a week of sightseeing and recreation.

The Estonians, Nordic and conservative by nature, were gracious hosts, but not nearly as warm as the Georgians. Sasha's efforts to cure my blues with all-night parties at the Estonian Central Committee *dacha* did not impress the house hostess, who thought we should be happy with mere-ly a beer or two after dinner. Sasha dragged me through every disco, night club, and variety show in Tallinn till sunrise. On my return to Moscow, I needed a vacation!

Tallinn was the start of what would prove to be a crazy streak in my life -- a reaction to knowing I was now permanently cut off from family and friends in the United States. I was alone, inside a new country, a new culture.

Returning to Moscow, I was told that my new *dacha* needed some roof work. They moved me back to my first *dacha*, next to Secretary Yeltsin. I lived alone, without accompaniment, but with four military guards down the road.

My movements were restricted because the area was considered "special" and I grew tired of not being able to walk or travel where and when I wanted to. I found the guards intimidating, but was told they were there for my protection. I did not feel free. Were they there to protect me —or control me?

One night in September I'd had quite enough solitude. I turned out the house lights to make the guards think I'd retired a bit early. Then, aware of the placement of infra-red alarm beams, I climbed over a fence and out of the compound. Finally, real freedom!

I walked fifteen minutes then found a car to take me into the center of Moscow. Alone at last, in the center of Moscow! But what could I do? I made my way to a night club in the basement of the Intourist Hotel, took in the show, had a few beers.

I met two Finnish nurses more drunk than I and invited them back to my *dacha* to continue our party. It was four in the morning. We found a taxi to take us to my *dacha*. I rang the gate bell and came face to face with one of my guards. He looked at me in astonishment.

"Ivan Ivanovitch!" he hollered. "What are you doing on the other side of the gate?"

I explained that I had come home with guests and to please let us in. He let me in, asked my girlfriends for their identification and called a KGB duty car to take them home.

As I expected, Victor dropped by the next day to inquire about the affair. I told him that nothing horrible had happened, and that I just wanted to be treated like everyone else —and go places without guards.

"In time you will," said Victor. "But for now you are in a very special place under special conditions. Please bear with us until next week, when you can return to your own *dacha*."

It took longer than week, more like two, but I was moved back to Zhukovka and Igor and Vladimir asked me what kind of career I wanted to follow. I told them I wanted nothing to do with intelligence; I wanted serious work in the areas of economics or finance. They promised to investigate work opportunities and keep me posted.

In October I learned that my mother, sister and sister's son planned to visit me in November. The Soviet consulate had sent them visas and airline tickets. My father wanted to come, too, but he was still working at Texas Instruments and we all felt it prudent that he wait.

I had been exchanging letters with my wife, and I noted conflicting themes in her letters. On one hand, Mary discussed the possibility of a divorce and the need for us both to start new lives. On the other, she made comments about certain special times we had shared together during our marriage and how she missed my company.

I was also confused about my feelings towards her. I wanted to see her and my son, but I was upset by her refusal to visit me and at least talk about our problems.

My mother's visit in November cleared up many mysteries and was very beneficial for me. Mom told me that Mary wanted very much to see me, but was under heavy pressure from the FBI and her family not to go to Moscow. Mom told me that Mary would try to visit me in the spring of 1987.

I couldn't meet my mother at the airport because the KGB did not want to risk a provocation. I waited at the *dacha* while Igor, Sasha and others welcomed her, my sister and my nephew at the airport. It was dark outside when they arrived at my *dacha* in a black Volga. My sister later told me that they were frightened at being driven into the woods during the night by Russian strangers.

My mother's eyes, and my own, filled with tears when we saw each other.

My friends provided my family with an English-speaking guide to show them Moscow's sights. Sometimes I stayed at home while they explored the city so I could baby-sit my nephew, Eric, almost the same age as my son. It made me realize what I had been missing as a father for more than a year. The experience made me wish even more that one day soon I would see my own son again.

Mom, Debra and Eric left in mid-November. Their departure left me little to do in the evenings except feel sorry for myself. Slowly, I felt myself slipping into another depression.

Vladimir introduced me to several officials of the Soviet Bank for Foreign Trade. They asked me to do financial research on a number of gold bond projects they were contemplating. I worked on these projects at my *dacha* during the day with materials provided by the bank. Interestingly, the terms and conditions of the gold bonds issued by the Russians in 1993 embodied my financial research.

One snowy night in late November, about 10 p.m., I left my *dacha* and walked to the train station, planning to catch a late train from Zhukovka into Moscow. I was now permitted to go places on my own, although my team preferred that I use a KGB car and driver. I had no particular plans in Moscow, but I was bored out of my skull at the *dacha*.

After waiting ten minutes on a platform as forlorn as myself, the lights of a police jeep shone upon me. A police officer got out and asked me what I was doing. I told him I was waiting for the train. He said all trains had been canceled due to heavy snow. He asked me for my identification documents.

Bureaucracies are the same the world over, I guess, and there had been a KGB screw-up on the identity papers they were supposed to give me. All I had on me was my U.S. diplomatic passport, which the U.S. government had never asked me to return. I handed it to the police officer and he told me that I was not authorized to be in this "special" area.

"You'll have to come with us," said the officer.

He ordered me into the vehicle and we drove to a police station three miles away.

The station commander lectured me. "Don't you know that's a special area and as an American you're not allowed to be there?"

"I'm a guest here," I said. "A guest of the KGB. I've got a *dacha*—and the KGB is protecting me."

"This is not likely and not funny, Mister Howard."

I pleaded with them to take me to my *dacha*, where the guards would recognize and vouch for me. They refused.

Forty-five minutes later, two fat men in their fifties arrived to look at me. They must have been from the ninth department of the KGB, which guarded government officials. They said they didn't know anything about me or any American guest in a *dacha*.

At 1 a.m. the police commander called the duty officer at the Ministry of Foreign Relations for instructions on what to do with me. They told him they would contact the American embassy and that the police should take me there.

I protested loudly, but the policemen threw me into the jeep. I swore at the police commander, but this only made him more determined to deliver me to the embassy. Until now, the whole thing had been mildly humorous, but now it was getting ridiculous—and I was scared. If they handed me over to the U.S. embassy, it would be the same as planting me in U.S. soil. They'd have me in a plane bound for Washington within hours.

During the 20-mile drive into downtown Moscow I considered jumping from the police car. We arrived at the U.S. embassy at 2 a.m. and the car stopped outside the Soviet guard station on the embassy's south side. U.S. Marine guards stood 20 yards away.

I got out. Four Soviet policemen surrounded me.

"That's your embassy," said one. "Go ahead in."

"I'm not going in," I said. "I'm going to get a taxi and go home to my *dacha*."

"You're not going anyplace but inside."

I tried to move away, but they began pushing me towards the main entrance on the east side of the building. We wrestled—me and half-a-dozen Soviet police.

"My name is Howard!" I, yelled in Russian, "I have the right of political asylum in Russia!"

One of the younger guards finally took a close look at me. Recognition. "He's right!" said the guard. "I saw him on television a couple of months ago!"

The policemen froze and stared at me.

The senior officer ordered me into the guard shack and made several phone calls to his superiors. I waited for what seemed like eternity while my fate was being decided. Sasha finally showed up near dawn. They looked pale and nervous.

"We are so lucky to have you back, Ed," said Sasha. "You gave us a scare."

"Gave you a scare?"

Igor came by the next morning. He was shaken by what had happened. "I'm responsible for you," he reminded me. "I would have been put in jail if they had forced you in there." He told me that KGB Chairman Victor Chebrikov had spoken to the Moscow chief of police to make sure this never happened again, and told me that I would be given local identification papers soon.

Later, Igor listened to a tape made of the phone call from the Soviet Ministry of Foreign Affairs duty officer to the Marine guard who answers the phone after hours at the U.S. embassy. The Ministry told the Marine guard in English that a Mr. Edward Lee Howard had been apprehended in a restricted area and was being brought to the embassy. The Marine either didn't understand or thought it was a joke, and twice hung up on the Soviet caller.

Igor decided I needed a trip someplace to rest and enjoy Christmas. He suggested one of the Baltic republics. I agreed that a trip was in order, but told him I didn't want to spend Christmas in the U.S.S.R., and I suggested visiting an Eastern European country such as Czechoslovakia, Poland, or Hungary.

Since my patron, General Kryuchkov, had served as a diplomat in Hungary under Ambassador (later KGB Chairman and General Secretary) Yuri V. Andropov during the 1956 revolt, Igor thought Hungary would be the best choice. He and I traveled to Budapest in mid-December and spent five weeks enjoying the "Paris of the East." I'll tell more about that trip shortly, but let me digress for a moment to better acquaint you with the man who helped me make the transition from an unemployed, depressed defector with a drinking problem to a well-adjusted (if sometimes lonely) productive citizen.

General Vladimir Aleksandrovitch Kryuchkov and I first met over dinner shortly after I first arrived in Moscow in September, 1985. When I met him, he was a Colonel General (three stars), and when he was promoted to head of the KGB, he became a four-star general. The last time we saw each other was before the 1991 putsch. Since the putsch we have sent messages of "hello and best regards" to each other via mutual acquaintances, but have deferred meeting because of a political climate unfavorable to him. He was one of the leaders of the 1991 attempt by conservatives to oust Mikhail Gorbachev and restore Communist rule. Boris Yeltsin reportedly wanted Kryuchkov shot. The two remain bitter foes.

General Kryuchkov has been like a strict grandfather to me. During our six years of regular contact, we had dinner together seven or eight times and he sent a number of gifts to me and my family. These ranged from the short-wave radio I used to hear news broadcasts when I first arrived in Moscow to English-language cartoon videos for my son on his visits.

He never tried to court my friendship. His gifts were never ostentatious, but were always practical, and his advice for me was always frank. He showed a genuine interest in my readjustment and in helping reunite me and my family.

In the first two years I lived in the Soviet Union, Kryuchkov was not at all impressed with my progress towards adjusting to my new life. He clearly wanted me to become a productive member of society wherever I ultimately settled. After I made it clear that I did not want to be involved with intelligence activities, he instructed his officers to introduce me to bankers, factory directors, and economic institutions with the goal of finding me interesting, productive work.

In my first months here, I complained that his guards would not even let me enjoy the simple freedom of a walk alone in the woods by my *dacha*. He changed that, and whether I was ever really alone or not, I at least had the pleasure of feeling alone during those troubled days. He strongly discouraged me from making my 1986 covert trip to the United States. Yet when he saw how critical it was for me to determine for myself whether or not my wife could be safely contacted, he had his best man train me, provide me with all the necessary counterfeit documents and had me flown to the Czech border in his personal jet.

On the other hand, Kryuchkov is a heavy-handed leader with the disposition of a feisty terrier. He comes from "the old school": those who developed their political ideology and work ethics during Stalin's regime. He ran the KGB as a tight ship and did not allow much room for debate. Officers who failed in their assignments were not coddled—they were punished. When Kryuchkov was in a room full of generals, they didn't speak until he spoke first.

He commanded the total respect of his officers, and his desire for total control inspired my idea to buy him a red riding stick (much the same kind that drill instructors carry) as a birthday present in 1988. I thought of it as a "gag" joke, but his officers later told me that he kept the stick in his office!

I only saw him lose his temper twice, and he was a man you didn't want to have mad at you. The first time was when I first met him and thanked his officers for their professionalism in getting me into the U.S.S.R. Kryuchkov was clearly upset when the Soviet embassy in Helsinki told me to go and relax for a couple of days while they checked with Moscow. He sent a blistering cable to Helsinki, reprimanding them for letting me out of their sight.

The second time I saw Kryuchkov lose control he looked like Nikita Khrushchev when Khruschev pounded the podium with his shoe during a speech at the United Nations in the early 1960s. I was having lunch with Victor Chebrikov (then Chairman of the KGB) and Kryuchkov at the clubhouse in Yasenevo in 1986. I made the mistake of mentioning Vitaly Yurchenko and his re-defection to the U.S.S.R.

Kryuchkov exploded and stood up at the table, shaking his fist at my mention of Yurchenko's name, roaring "You are not Yurchenko. You cannot return. I have punished him!"

I have no doubt that this statement was purely spontaneous, but an intelligence analyst could interpret it in two different ways. Either the message was meant to convince me that I could not return to the United States because Yurchenko's defection and re-defection were both staged by the KGB, or that Yurchenko's antics were spontaneous, and that he had been punished for them.

We may never know which, but I believe that Yurchenko was punished. What I know for certain is that Kryuchkov has a hot temper and short fuse when Yurchenko's name is mentioned.

My conversations with Kryuchkov consisted of ten percent speaking and ninety percent listening. Even with my

Russian language skills, I found it hard to get a word in. This was partly because he was briefed by his officers on my status before each meeting and knew what was on my mind.

My relationship with Vladimir Kryuchkov was very personal, and that's unusual in the intelligence business. In the 1970s and 1980s, for example, the CIA developed a bad reputation among defectors: For the first few months, the CIA would treat a defector like a prince while pumping him for information. But after sucking him dry, they'd boot him out the back door with a few hundred dollars a month to keep him off welfare and a phone number to call if he got into trouble.

Kryuchkov treated me and my family well, and I will always be grateful for that. Did his humanitarian treatment of me spring from inside him, or was it a payback motivated by hidden guilt that I had taken so much heat for Aldrich Ames as a result of the Yurchenko defection?

He may have had a guilt complex about me. He was running Aldrich Ames, and he knew I was taking the blame every time an American intelligence officer was arrested and each time the KGB burned and arrested another agent in Russia. I'd tune in to the "Voice of America" and hear radio broadcasts blaming me, and my KGB friends would laugh and say, "Well, Ivan, you did it again!"

Ames was providing the information, and I was taking the hits. Kryuchkov knew this. I'll never know for certain his motives, but I like to think they were personal, not just professional.

Kryuchkov knew everything. He is writing his own book, but I doubt he'll tell all. He's of the old, honorable school, unlike the "new school" in Russia, which will sell anything to anybody for five hundred dollars.

Chapter Seventeen

Coming Together

Moscow is oddly seductive, like a cranky lover. Daily life creates a buildup of frustrations: the potholes in the streets, the slow-moving Russian bureaucracy. But when I take business trips, it is always a pleasure to return to the Russian capital. I have my *dacha*, my friends, my routine, and visits from my family. Moscow grows on you. If you talk to people who have lived in Moscow and left, you'll find most of them wish to return. Sure, while they're here they whine and bitch and moan. But they all fight to get back.

Budapest in December was a pleasant contrast to Moscow. The Hungarian equivalent of the KGB met Igor and me at the airport and drove us to a middle-class guest house. I still did not possess a new passport, but my host, Istvan, said it did not matter. Istvan apologized for the accommodations, saying "We were told only that a guest from Moscow would arrive. We did not know it was you, Mr. Howard." I was flattered. Later we drove to a modern, two-bedroom villa in the northern part of Budapest.

Igor returned to Moscow after Christmas, but I stayed on until the third week of January, 1987. I roamed the city, getting to know it, searching for business opportunities and making friends.

Hildy, the villa's hostess, was an excellent cook. She prepared the kind of spicy food I missed from Santa Fe. Unlike "godless Moscow," Budapest was festive over Christmas. People shopped; the churches were decorated.

On Christmas Eve I attended to mass at Saint Istvan's Cathedral. I fell in love with Budapest during this trip, and felt it would make a good home for me, my wife and son.

I phoned Mary several times and conveyed my excitement about Budapest. She seemed friendlier, took an interest, and this gave me some hope. Between Christmas and New Years, I built up the courage to invite Mary to meet me in Budapest.

She said yes. Thrilled, I raced home to tell Hildy. Mary would come alone. I was disappointed that my son would not come, too, but Mary wanted time alone with me to see if things could be worked out, and I understood this. Budapest was an ideal venue for our meeting because it was less threatening politically than Moscow.

With these new developments, my future began to look bright. I was safe in a comfortable city, I had friends—and Mary was finally coming to see me.

My euphoria was short lived. Within a week, Mary called in tears. She had been visited by the FBI and CIA, who demanded that she "voluntarily surrender" her U.S. passport to prevent her from visiting me. I was pissed!

Amerika! So much for the "land of the free." The U.S. government had no legal right to deny my wife her freedom to travel. Again, they couldn't get me, so they targeted my family, keeping us separated for political reasons. When other countries attempt such tactics, the U.S.A. protests loudly.

I swore vengeance. Istvan was afraid I'd do something stupid at the U.S. embassy in Budapest. Igor flew in from Moscow to calm me down. He told me I would win the battle for my family with "patience and not with stupidity."

I settled for inviting my sister and her son join me at Hildy's villa for a week. Their company helped relieve the anguish I suffered from the denial of my wife's visit.

Igor and I returned to Moscow in late January. Igor assured me that we'd try to invite her to Moscow -- and that the Soviet government would mount an international media barrage if the U.S. government denied her travel a second time.

I phoned my wife on her birthday in February and again invited her to visit me. She said she would request the return of her passport. I made it clear to her—and the FBI, listening through their tap—that the Soviets were prepared to make a media issue of the affair if her passport was not returned.

Whether it was my phone speech, some back-channel communications between the Soviets and the Americans, or the realization at the State Department that withholding her passport was illegal, Mary's passport was returned to her.

Mary told me in March that she and Lee, and my mother, would travel to Moscow in April. I rejoiced.

Igor and Sasha collected my wife, son and mother at the airport. I sent a bouquet of roses along for them, with a card that said—at Igor's suggestion—"From Russia with Love."

The car stopped at my *dacha* I saw my son jump out. My heart soared.

"Hello, Daddy," he said.

I couldn't talk immediately because of a large lump in my throat. It had been nineteen months since I had seen my wife and son. To see them now, after what I'd been through—after what they'd been through—was overwhelming.

I hugged my son. And then my wife. We were a family again.

Mary and I got on like two old friends. We renewed our relationship and discussed what had happened during the past year-and-a-half. We took walks through the *dacha* gardens and slowly caught up with each other. After re-hashing the past, we discussed the future and its possibilities.

Mary could not conceive of a life outside of the United States, yet she seemed interested in reuniting our family on a permanent basis.

I proposed that we visit Budapest together. Mary accepted, but she expressed doubt that our marriage could ever work again. We all flew to Budapest, after one week in Moscow, at the invitation of the Hungarian government. Much to my delight, we stayed in Hildy's guest house. She and Mary hit it off instantly. Hildy's desserts were a strong argument for living there. At the end of the week, Mary decided to extend her stay for several days. She liked Budapest. She liked being free to roam the city without international pressures upon us. Mary wanted a normal, quiet life; neither Moscow nor Washington were her cup of tea. For my part, I concentrated on being a good husband and father again.

My time with Lee was a great learning experience. I had left him when he was two-and-a-half years-old and now he was four. He could now express himself well, and he asked me questions about what I did and why I didn't work in the United States. I told him I was a businessman and that my work was here for now. It was my plan to explain the whole situation to him when he became a teenager.

I was very sorry to see my family depart for the United States in early May. My mother told me she was sure that, with patience, the emotional wounds would heal. Mary agreed to return in late summer and try living together again on a temporary basis. We agreed to take it one step at a time.

I flew to Moscow and made arrangements to return to Hungary in late June. I would need a permanent place to live in Budapest and something productive to do. The pieces of my life were coming back together.

Chapter Eighteen

Budapest

And so I was moving—to Budapest.

Concerned for my security, General Kryuchkov gave me a list of Soviet embassy personnel. I would use my Soviet diplomatic passport for travel and, once there, my name would be Scott Alan Roth.

I packed up my possessions in Moscow and returned to Budapest on June 13, 1987. The Hungarian KGB hosted me at Hildy's villa for a week—time enough to find a temporary apartment.

Budapest was hot and muggy that summer, so I was fortunate to find an apartment in the hills, above the city, where I could catch a breeze.

The Hungarian KGB helped me obtain an Austrian driver's license under my alias, and I bought a used BMW.

In July, writer David Wise visited Budapest to spend five days interviewing me for his book, *The Spy Who Got Away.* I met with him because, after months of character assassination, I wanted to show that I wasn't Darth Vader.

I discussed meeting Wise with my friends in the KGB. They were against it, but they had a reasonable position: "If it's important to you, go ahead and do it, but let's talk about what you are going to say first."

To account for the time when I was in Moscow unofficially, we fabricated a legend that I had been traveling in Latin America and Europe. I would say that I didn't arrive in Moscow until June of 1986, and that I did so via an unnamed Socialist country, which he deduced was Hungary.

I also kept from Wise the classified duties I was to have undertaken for the CIA in Moscow. Had I disclosed this information, federal attorneys could say that even if I hadn't disclosed secrets to the KGB, I disclosed them to Wise. At that point, I wasn't sure where I would live. I didn't rule out returning to the United States.

I have mixed feelings about what Wise wrote in his book about me. On one hand, his book offered me an opportunity to tell my side of the story. On the other, I was quoted out of context a number of times and he made a number of allegations that had no basis in fact.

During the summer I discovered the British embassy library in Budapest. Starved for English-language reading material, I spent countless hours in the library. It was there that I first read about George Blake, the British MI6 officer and Soviet spy who escaped to Moscow in the mid-1960s. I was fascinated that he was able to escape after six years in a British prison and secretly make his way to Moscow. I had the good fortune to meet George in Moscow several years ago, and I number him among my closest friends.

The British Embassy Club was located next to the embassy library, and a member invited me in one evening after the library closed. It was a small club that featured darts and good ale, and I found myself attracted to the place on Fridays because I was lonely and because I enjoyed chatting in my mother tongue. My reasons for going there were strictly social.

One evening at the club I met an American couple who were living in Budapest. The husband was working on contract to service helicopters for the Hungarian government. His wife Connie invited me to the Canadian Embassy

Club the following week. I thanked her but said I expected to be out of town. From a security standpoint, cultivating Americans as friends was imprudent.

Nonetheless, the following week, with little else to do, I drove to the Canadian embassy and entered the club. My apprehensions were put to rest by the friendly Canadians, happy to find a new western face in town. Connie appeared later and, again, had an interesting chat. I trusted this tall, blond woman and developed a friendly, platonic relationship with her that summer. She knew my wife was coming and promised to introduce Mary to other Western women when she arrived.

Meanwhile, Sasha had been posted to Budapest for two years as a Soviet consular officer and had moved his family to town. Naturally, one of his jobs was to keep an eye on me and ensure that I was safe. We had weekly meetings in one of the many pastry shops downtown. When I told him about the Canadian Embassy Club and Connie, he warned me against continuing such activities. "Moscow will not be happy to hear that you are not taking your security seriously," he told me. I thanked him for his concern, but told him that my security was my responsibility and that I felt no threat.

Later that summer, I met a U.S. embassy communications clerk at the Canadian club. He was an older man, about to be posted to Turkey. Despite the fact that he processed all of the embassy's secret cables, I made no attempt to cultivate any relationship with him, although I did share a few beers with him on occasion. I mentioned him to Sasha one day. Sasha nearly went berserk.

"Do you know how long and how hard we'd have to work to meet such a man? All our careers and more! And you walk in the door and drink beer with him. That's great! Tell me about him!"

"Forget him. He's leaving next week for Turkey," I said. "Are you still against my visiting the club?" I smiled.

Sasha was disappointed, but he never ceased asking me about new Western personalities I met in Budapest. Unfortunately for him, I never met another cipher clerk.

Mary and Lee arrived in Budapest in August for a three-month stay. Connie befriended Mary and gave her several orientation tours. Mary and I searched for a school for Lee and settled on the American International School, which had a kindergarten program. We enrolled him, starting September. By this time, we had moved to a house in the nearby village of Szentendre, near Budapest.

Lee liked his new school and his British teacher. Mary occupied herself making friends among the wives of Budapest's international community. I began my search for a job in international trade.

November came upon us swiftly and, with it, Lee and Mary's return to return the United States. I closed up our house in the village and spent the holidays at my *dacha* in Zhukovka.

I learned from Igor a few months earlier that the East German Security Service (the *Stazi*) was making a film to commemorate the fortieth anniversary of the CIA. They wanted me to visit East Berlin and be interviewed. I declined. I did not want to antagonize the American government. Maybe, I theorized, if I kept my nose clean, the U.S. government would let me live in peace. I still had hope for this in those days.

Now, with my family gone, and Igor still pressing me, I accepted the East German invitation, with the stipulation that I would not be filmed or recorded. They agreed and I traveled with Sasha to East Berlin.

A large *Stazi* jet flew Sasha, me and my two hosts in first class-style to East Berlin. A fleet of cars awaited our arrival. I sat in the back of a dark blue Volvo limousine with a senior *Stazi* official named Wolfgang and my interpreter. Sasha rode in one of the two escort cars, each full of guards carrying Uzi machine pistols. Wherever we drove, the guards blocked off traffic at the intersections or used their sirens and blue lights to clear a path. My driver played Jefferson Starship and Abba tapes on the stereo as we toured the city.

I was driven to a large, comfortable house and given a suite of rooms overlooking a river. The house had a large sauna, a billiard table and a refrigerator stocked with German beer. Mealtimes were formal, and as a country boy I didn't like a wearing a jacket and tie with every meal, but the food was top flight.

I told the guards that I liked to jog; a group of them appeared each morning to run with me. The guards were young and athletic, and seemed to enjoy my company compared with the old politicians they usually guarded. My jogging partners had dual assignments: to protect me—and to prevent me from running all the way into West Berlin if I had a fancy to re-defect.

My hosts offered me all the usual tourist attractions, and added that they would like to talk with me about the CIA. We developed a program that included a visit to Potsdam, several museums, some shopping and dinner at several good restaurants. Slots were left free for relaxation and for "chats" about the CIA.

It appeared that someone had mistakenly suggested I was eager to work with them and full of hard information—or they assumed this on their own. The "chats," to my dismay, turned into professional debriefing sessions—or at least that's what the *Stazi* wanted, digging for hard information on specific operations of which I had no knowledge. I had spent only two months on a rotational assignment at the CIA's German desk in 1982, and I couldn't have helped the *Stazi* even if I had wanted to. Hence, the East Germans were extremely upset that I had nothing to tell them.

An interesting incident took place while I was visiting Potsdam, where Germany's territory was carved up among the Allies at the end of World War II. At the end of the tour we noticed two men in military uniforms about 300 yards from us snapping photographs. Closer observation revealed them to be an American military officer with his aide. (They were driving an American car with special status license plates.)

My guards instructed me to turn from the camera and get in the limousine. We drove off and the Americans jumped into their car and followed us.

Wolfgang communicated by radio to our guards. He instructed them to detain the "Yankees" and take their cameras. I knew this could lead to a fight if the Americans resisted, and although I had taken a lot of hits from Washington during the past two years, I felt sorry for the guys in the American car. They were just doing their job, and I didn't want to see them get punched.

So I intervened and asked Wolfgang not to stop the Americans, but to ask one of our guard cars to block them while we sped ahead. In five minutes, the escapade was literally behind us.

Back in East Berlin, I was under more pressure to talk about the CIA. After four days, I'd had enough. I told Sasha I wanted to go home to Moscow. He understood. Wolfgang was upset, and asked me to stay one day longer and have dinner with the East German Deputy Security Minister. As a courtesy, I agreed. Then I departed—and I was much happier alone in my *dacha* wearing blue jeans than having official dinners with hosts who wanted only to discuss the CIA.

Lee and Mary arrived in Moscow a week late because my son didn't want to leave the comforts of his family and friends in Minnesota. I was upset, but Mary said it was natural, and that he just needed more time to get used to me and our situation in Hungary.

Our threesome returned to Budapest in January, 1988. Lee went back to school, Mary got involved in the International Women's Club, and I looked for work. Mary remarked that our old friend Connie was not as friendly as before.

I thought this was strange, but I later discovered what had happened: the U.S. embassy became aware of my presence in Budapest, and they had spread the word among the American expatriate community not to socialize with us. I could understand placing a quarantine around me, but I never saw why this should extend to my family members.

From the first time Mary and Lee had arrived in Budapest, I stayed away from the embassy clubs, so as to keep them "clean" for my wife and son. Moreover, I didn't want any foreign embassy to protest to the Hungarians about my activities. Mary shared my concerns. She collected Lee from school on her own, and she limited her social activities to non-American women.

I eventually found part-time consulting work with a Hungarian-Swiss firm that evaluated investments for foreign concerns.

In late spring, Mary, Lee and I rode a train from Budapest to Kiev. The Soviets tried to teach my wife how to drink vodka "parachutist style": hold 2 ounces in your mouth for thirty seconds before swallowing! Lee enjoyed touring the War Museum and fishing on the Dnieper river.

I was taken alone on a special excursion to Chernobyl, and I visited the nuclear power plant that had hemorrhaged in

1986. I also visited the town—now a ghost-town—outside the plant. It was the eeriest experience of my life, seeing deserted houses with toys still in the yard, not an animal in sight. There were many graves where soldiers and firemen who had fought lay buried.

Following a brief stay in Moscow, we traveled to one of the true wonders of the world: the magnificent Lake Baikal in Siberia. Unfortunately, getting there is not half the fun. It entails seven hours on Aeroflot, the world's worst airline.

Mary and Lee returned to the United States in the autumn, and I killed time in Moscow. I noticed a difference in people's attitudes towards politics. *Glasnost* and *svabodnost* (openness and freedom) were now hot topics on the street. I met average citizens who talked openly about changing the system—people who would never before have discussed such matters openly. The KGB officers I knew were about evenly divided as to whether democratic changes would be good or bad. Some thought it was time for the old guard to step down and bring in new faces; others feared the changes would lead to a polarization of society. I kept my opinions to myself, maintaining that I was not a political person. Secretly, I wanted some change but I still felt like an outsider and thought it best not to advocate any position.

Reunited again in Budapest, my family resumed our normal activates: school for Lee, part-time work for me, and homemaking for my wife. We moved to an apartment nearer Lee's school and I got involved with a Hungarian-Spanish-German joint-venture to launch a tourist restaurant and produce a local beer.

The year 1988 was good for us. We were together in Hungary, living like a normal family. Mary and Lee remained with me for Christmas, and everything seemed fine. We didn't know it, but an ill wind was heading our way from Washington.

Chapter Nineteen

Troubled Horizon

Moscow is full of fascinating people. In the spring of 1989 I met two of them: ex-spy George Blake, and General Leonid Vladimiravitch Shebarshin, Kryuchkov's replacement as chief of the First Directorate of the KGB.

George Blake is the only western spy I have ever met in Russia. Once an officer in Britain's MI6, Blake was convicted in the 1960s of spying for Russia. He escaped from Wormwood Scrubs prison in 1966 and had been living in Moscow for twenty-three years when I met him.

At our first lunch, in my *dacha*, Blake personified the proper English gentleman. He wore a suit, a bow tie and sported a carefully-trimmed beard. Blake was and still is a communist. He crossed to the Soviets for ideological reasons. I asked him, "Now that the Soviet Union has crumbled, why do you stay here?"

"Well, for better or worse, I'm kind of married to this place," he told me.

At our first meeting, Blake and I spent hours talking about the problems we had adapting to life in the Soviet Union. He, as I, found separation from our families and finding meaningful work were the main challenges.

"The most important thing," he told me, "is finding good work. Your family is all right and they can survive without you. You could make a life here without them if you had to, but you could not survive without meaningful work."

Blake told me that his three grown sons from England visit him, and he remarked on how lucky he was to find a good marriage partner, Ida, in the Soviet Union.

I never met any of the other Soviet spies who lived in and around Moscow. The KGB wanted me to meet Kim Philby in 1986, but I declined. Philby was an ideologue, a dedicated Communist, and I'm not. I didn't think there was any point meeting him. But after getting to know George Blake, I regret that decision. Philby and I would have found common ground on adjusting to life in Russia.

I finally agreed to meet Philby in spring of 1988. But on my return from Budapest the KGB told me he was in the hospital. A month later he was dead.

For all the publicity they generate when they arrive, Moscow's community of intelligence defectors is amazingly small.

Marcus Wolff, former head of East German intelligence, resided less than a mile from my *dacha*, in Zhukova, in 1991. He wasn't happy. He lasted about six months, then turned himself in to the West Germans.

Glenn Michael Souther defected to Moscow secretly via Prague in 1986. He was a former U.S. Navy enlisted man who worked with satellite imaging and intelligence. I learned he was here through General Kryuchkov who, over dinner, said, "Yes, Mike has gotten married, has a daughter, and he's teaching English." I told the KGB that I'd like to meet him, and they approved. I also heard from my guards that he wanted to meet me.

Souther was extremely interested in the Soviet poet Mayakovsky, who died under mysterious circumstances. The next thing I heard, Souther had committed suicide. That was the summer of 1989.

Just before the collapse of the Berlin Wall, the West German counterintelligence chief, Tietke, defected to East Germany, for whom he had been secretly working. Later, he moved to Moscow with his wife, and the Russians built him a *dacha* in Sochi, on the Black Sea—the Miami Beach of Russia.

James Bond fans would not be disappointed with General Leonid Vladimiravitch Shebarshin. A polished, well-educated professional intelligence officer, Shebarshin has dark, handsome features and speaks perfect English. He rose through the ranks to senior spymaster in the KGB. Shebarshin learned the spy trade in Pakistan and India—and made his mark running KGB operations in Afghanistan. Kryuchkov picked him for his brilliance in operations—one of the few times that a professional intelligence officer took over the First Directorate instead of a politician from the Central Committee of the Communist Party.

I met General Shebarshin and several of his aides at a dinner given for me in a *dacha* at Yasnevo. He congratulated me on behalf of General Kryuchkov for my success with adapting to life in Hungary.

"We are all glad to see you together with your family, and we are glad that you are happy and healthy," toasted Shebarshin.

He then invited me to travel to Nicaragua and Cuba that summer as the special guest of the KGB Resident Officers, and to visit Afghanistan with him in the fall. I readily accepted the first offer; I have always maintained a special fondness for Latin America. I also accepted the second offer, though it puzzled me because I knew that the Soviets were thinking of pulling out of Afghanistan.

I was impressed by Shebarshin and wanted to get to know him better. He quoted Thomas Jefferson and had a good feel for what made Americans tick. I'll describe the trips to Cuba and Nicaragua shortly; the trip to Afghanistan never materialized. General Kryuchkov, one of the leaders of the 1991 putsch, was arrested after the plot failed, and Shebarshin ran the KGB for only a week. He was ousted because of his closeness to Kryuchkov. This was a loss for Russia; Shebarshin would have made a fine KGB chief. Today he is a respected security consultant to the Russian and European banking community.

On my return to Budapest in the summer of 1989, I set about finalizing the documents approving my participation in my joint venture. Then appeared a stumbling block: Hungarian law required that I have a company listed in the commercial register of my native country in order to legally participate in a Hungarian business. I doubted that the U.S. embassy would be of any help!

Sasha and my host, George, an Hungarian KGB officer, argued about how to obtain commercial registration for me. Moscow wanted the Hungarians to fake the registration papers and the Hungarians wanted Moscow to fake the papers. Two years earlier, the Hungarians would have dared not argue the point. But now there was a wind of change blowing throughout socialist Europe. The Hungarian Parliament was calling for less KGB activity and more western investment in Hungary.

After strong pressure from Kryuchkov in Moscow, the Hungarian KGB presented me with fake commercial registration papers, which I presented to the Hungarian Court of Registration for participation in the project. The papers consisted of a sworn statement by a notary public in New York certifying that he had filed my company's registration papers. Later, Sasha confided to me that the Soviet KGB was adamant that the Hungarians should do the forgery, in case a scandal broke and the fake papers were discovered. This demonstrates the paranoia that was growing among the various socialist intelligence agencies in the late 1980s.

Mary and Lee returned to the United States in the summer of 1989 to visit Mary's family. I flew to Moscow for a two-week visit before departing to Cuba and Nicaragua. Kryuchkov was adamant that I not be allowed to set foot for even a second in a country not under his influence. This ruled out most of Aeroflot's flights to Cuba because they stopped to refuel in Canada. They finally found a non-stop flight from East Berlin to Havana. Accompanied by a friendly KGB officer named Nik, I flew from East Berlin to Havana in July, 1989.

We were met by two Cuban intelligence officers from the *Direccion Generale de Inteligencia* (DGI) in a chauffeured Mercedes limousine. They drove us to a charming house near the beach on the eastern side of Havana.

I spent a week in Cuba, sightseeing, sampling the cuisine, fishing for barracuda and generally enjoying myself. Havana was poor, but in 1989, at least, most of its people seemed happy and committed to Fidel Castro.

The night clubs, and the Ernest Hemingway bar, abounded with European and Canadian tourists. I thought it a shame that Americans couldn't enjoy the pristine beaches and carefree night life, so close to their own shores.

The Cuban DGI officers were pleased that I still remembered how to speak Spanish. Our conversations were mostly social, since I had no experience at the CIA's Latin American division and knew nothing about the Cuban desk. The major complaint that the Cubans had against the Americans was Radio Marti, a U.S. government television station that beamed programming at Cuba.

By KGB standards, I found the DGI officers informal. I remember when the DGI's chief of counter-intelligence arrived for a dinner at the beach house. He was a Cuban general, and was accompanied by another Cuban from the same section who held the rank of colonel. After a couple of

Cuba Libres (rum and cola), the talk turned to attempts to recruit CIA personnel. The colonel became so excited that he sat on the armrest of the general's chair. Nik and I exchanged grins at this show of informality which, had it happened in Moscow, would have denied the junior officer any hope of future promotion.

The Cubans posed an interesting question to me while I was in Havana. They said that they had identified a female CIA officer involved in lesbian activities. They wondered if they should confront her with this knowledge and blackmail her into cooperation with them. They asked my opinion.

I reflected for a few moments on the way that the CIA had unceremoniously cashiered me. I told the Cubans that they'd be better off to advise the woman that it would be only a matter of time before the CIA found out about her and threw her out in the cold without even a thank you note for her service.

"Tell her that cooperating with the DGI now could help insure her retirement pension," I told them. "Because there will be none from the CIA when they become aware of her sexual preference."

The DGI general considered this for a minute.

"*Que buen pase!*" (What a good pass!), he said, using a phrase usually used to describe a graceful movement by a matador in the bull ring.

I was asked about "how the typical CIA officer thinks." They were curious not only about how the typical CIA officers approaches intelligence problems, but also about his working relationships with the CIA station chief in the U.S. embassy and the respective country desks at Langley.

The DGI also asked me how the average CIA officer viewed recruitment of agents. They wanted to know if the CIA had a gung-ho attitude toward recruitment, or whether they were suspicious of possible informers. This seemed like a ridiculous question, because I knew that CIA officers were promoted or not promoted by the number of agents they recruited. The rule in the academic world is, "publish or perish." In the CIA, it's "recruit or retire as a GS-10."

Nik and I flew to Nicaragua aboard Cubana Airlines. Daniel Ortega and the Sandanistas were still in power, and I looked forward to visiting a country I had not seen since leaving the Peace Corps sixteen years earlier.

Our plane dived steeply at Managua to avoid ground-to-air missiles. We were met by a squad of Soviet KGB officers armed with automatic weapons.

My hostess was Maria, an alluring, dark-haired, brown-eyed woman in her twenties. She looked more like a movie star than a lieutenant in the Nicaraguan Security Forces. Maria was my personal escort for a week. She showed Nik and me the sights of Managua, and took us to the northern provinces where Contra activity was taking place.

Unlike Havana, Managua had little night life. We spent evenings in the garden of our cottage, conversing with our hosts. Ultimately, with their country deeply entrenched in civil war, the Nicaraguans had little to offer me. We returned to Havana and grabbed a flight back to East Berlin.

As we left the Havana airport, the Cuban DGI officers took Nik's camera, developed his film and cut out any shots of themselves.

Mary and Lee joined me in Budapest in mid-August. Several weeks later, I received a request from Kryuchkov to consult with him in Moscow. I asked Sasha what was up, but he knew nothing. They requested only three days of my time: one to fly there, one for dinner with Kryuchkov, the third to return home. They sent me an airline ticket and I flew to Moscow.

I saw Nik first, and he was tight-lipped about the reasons for my invitation. "It's better," he said, "if Vladimir Aleksandrovitch [Kryuchkov] tells you himself."

At the Senior KGB Officers Club behind Lubyanka, Kryuchkov welcomed us. We sat down for drinks. Kryuchkov didn't mince words.

"The Hungarians have asked me to talk to you about leaving," he said. "There are great political pressures in Budapest which do not bode well for your future there. The Americans are gaining influence in the government, and your presence there could lead to a scandal which would be bad for you and our friends there. Don't worry. We understand that you want to continue living with your family outside Moscow, and we will help you find another place to live, perhaps in the German Democratic Republic or Czechoslovakia."

I was stunned. I had spent the past two years putting my life and family back together. Now I had to take everything apart and move elsewhere. My work, Mary's friends and Lee's schooling—all up in smoke. The beast had surfaced again: "The Americans are gaining influence," Kryuchkov had said.

I regained my composure to negotiate a departure date. I told the General that I had just brought my family back to Budapest, had recently started work, and my son was enrolled for another year of school.

"Yes, I understand," Kryuchkov said, "and I will write a letter tomorrow asking that you be permitted to stay in Budapest until next May, when your son's school term is complete. I think the Hungarians will understand."

Kryuchkov was not his usual self. He asked for my opinion on the political situation in Hungary and I told him that I thought the Hungarians wanted to court the West but were afraid of offending Moscow.

"You are correct on both points," he said. "The Hungarians are motivated by economic reasons, specifically the money promised to them. They are afraid of offending us, yes, but they should not fear us. We are fighting amongst ourselves here in Moscow, and do not have the teeth we should have in our foreign affairs."

I returned to Budapest and faced Mary with the bad news.

A few weeks later, in September, an Englishman sat next to me in a restaurant where I was eating alone. He struck up a conversation. I let my guard down and was friendly with him.

Within a few minutes, he asked me if I was Edward Howard. I froze. Then I admitted I was. He introduced himself as a British newspaper correspondent and asked if he could do an interview with me. I declined the offer and told the man I just wanted a quiet life and to be left alone. As I walked out of the restaurant, I noticed a blue German Ford that had been parked close to my house earlier that day. I realized this chance encounter with the correspondent had been no fluke. It was a set-up. My address was on file at the American International School. I felt the long arm of the CIA at work.

Two days later, Sasha phoned and wanted to meet me right away. He came to my apartment and told me what had happened.

"That so-called correspondent went to the U.S. ambassador and asked questions about your status here," Sasha said. "The U.S. ambassador then made a protest to the Hungarian Central Committee about your presence, and hinted strongly that your continued presence here could endanger a $160 million aid package the Americans were proposing for Hungary."

That was the CIA's plan of attack. Sasha said the Hungarians wanted to talk with me the next day. I knew then that the game was over for us in Budapest. The next day I told the Hungarian officials that I didn't want to cause any trouble. I wanted my son to finish the winter semester at his school, and we agreed to leave the country by the end of the year instead of the following May.

A week later, another surprise. The director of the American International School phoned my wife and invited her to a private conference. Mary returned very angry.

"They say they want Lee out of the school as soon as possible," she said. "The U.S. embassy representative on the school board believes Lee's presence could cause some negative press for the school. The director agreed with him."

"Yes," I replied. "And I bet that the U.S. embassy press officer will personally initiate the negative press if nobody else does."

Mary and the school director agreed that Lee would withdraw by December, just two months away. The request was not based on logic, but purely politics. This plot had clearly been cooked up by the CIA and the State Department.

I was angry, again, at Langley for targeting my family— and I was also angry with the Hungarian government. Sasha called them "political prostitutes." He promised that Moscow would find me and my family a new place to live.

"Easily said," I thought. "But where?" East Germany was out of the question; it would soon be a western state. Poland was also full of pro-Western sympathies. Cuba was a possibility, but it was a poor country and I did not want to subject Mary and Lee to its harsh living conditions. The Balkan countries (Yugoslavia, Romania and Albania) were also out of the question because of food shortages and unfavorable living conditions.

Czechoslovakia was the logical choice.

Sasha arranged for all of us to visit Prague for a week in late October. The Czechs provided us with a car, a driver and a guide. The Czech Deputy Minister of Security told me I could work with the Czech Foreign Investment Council. He said not to worry about Prague's commitment to social-ism or a repeat performance of what had happened in Budapest.

However, the Czechs did not want my son to attend the international school (which had Americans on the board) and the Soviets were proposing to send him an English-speaking tutor from the Soviet embassy.

Mary and I were skeptical about this. It would cut our son off from social contact with other children. But, ultimately, we found Prague a delight, and we wanted to keep our family together. So we agreed to move to Prague in Decem-ber.

The Hungarians handled our forced departure in a civil manner. They arranged for a diplomatic truck to transport our household effects to Prague. We spent much of Novem-ber packing and saying good-bye to our Hungarian friends, all of whom were puzzled by our departure. I told them simply that I'd been offered an interesting, profitable job in Prague.

Our impending arrival in Prague converged with some unsettling news: Vaclav Havel, the dissident writer, was preparing to take power amid talk of a "velvet revolution."

I relayed my concern to Sasha.

"You can be sure," he replied, "that we will stand behind you and protect your security."

"Oh, great," I thought. "Here we go again!" I didn't know where Czech politics were headed, and hoped only that my family could stay together a few years longer.

What the Czech Deputy Minister of Security had told me was impossible, was possible after all: Communism in Czechoslovakia was toppled.

Hopeful but cautious, we made our move to Prague in December, as planned. The Czechs moved us into a huge house with gardens in an affluent suburb of the city. Mary and I both felt it was too big, but we were delighted with the new environment. Prague was full of interesting museums and parks and superb restaurants.

A kind Russian woman named Natalia arrived each morning to tutor Lee. I was told to wait until after the New Year to discuss my new work, so I spent the time with Mary, organizing the house and buying furniture and accessories to make our new home more comfortable.

On New Year's Day I listened to an English-language broadcast on Radio Prague and a commentator blasted the communist officials for corruption and leading the country into ruin. I'd never heard such strong language on any public broadcast in any socialist country. I began to worry seriously about the implication this might have on my presence.

I called Sergei, my local Soviet contact, to stop by for a chat. He was anything but reassuring.

Sergei confirmed my worst fears. Czech politics had changed so dramatically so quickly that the Ministry of Security had sent its most sensitive files to the Soviet embassy and these were being shipped to a Soviet military base for safe-keeping. The officials with whom I'd met in October now feared for their own jobs, and had no time to find one for me. Sergei advised me to keep a low profile and sit tight. He said that Sasha would come from Budapest to discuss my situation.

Sasha arrived in mid-January and told me the bad news. Life, he said, would be impossible for me in Prague. General Kryuchkov asked me to consider moving my family to Moscow for my own protection.

Mary and I talked over the Moscow option. We agreed that Moscow was out of the question for Lee. He didn't speak

Russian, and we both wanted him to attend a normal school where English was the primary language.

I met with Sasha about this. I asked him about Cuba, and asked if we could organize a scouting party to Havana.

We left for Havana in February of 1990. Again, we flew non-stop from East Berlin again. The Cubans housed us in a beach resort house as they had on my previous trip. They took a special liking to Mary, who spoke Spanish from her years in the Peace Corps and our two years in Peru. On her birthday in February, they pampered her with flowers and a fine dinner replete with serenading musicians.

A visit to the international school left us disappointed, because English was poorly spoken. We were shown some nice houses for rent, but they were expensive at $2,000 a month in rent. And they needed renovations—at the lessor's expense—to bring them up to western standards. Poverty was rampant. I didn't want Mary and Lee to pay this price for my war with the FBI and CIA.

I asked the Cuban DGI officers if they had given consideration to the reaction of the American government to my possible relocation to Cuba. They told me that their foreign ministry had written a negative memo on the subject to Fidel Castro. The memo stated that our arrival would "anger the American government."

The DGI officers laughed when they told me Castro's response to the memo. "Nothing I do pleases the Americans," Castro had apparently said. "If Howard wants to live here, that's his choice."

I am not a Communist, but I do admire men who stick to their principles, and Fidel is one of them. His attitude was in sharp contrast to the sell-out situations I encountered in Hungary and Czechoslovakia.

Mary, Lee and I returned to Prague late in February. My wife and I took long walks and discussed the pros and cons of the decision before us. There were only two options: life together in Havana; or life apart.

Mary had her family and friends in America, and I knew that she missed them. She left the decision up to me. And I decided that she and Lee should return to the United States where Lee could attend a good school. Tears welled in her eyes.

I made the necessary reservations for Mary and Lee to return to the United States in mid-March. I planned to pack up and return to Moscow by the end of the month.

Our last week together in Prague was difficult for me. I kept looking at my wife and son, wondering how I would get along without them—and how they would be without me to look after them. Their material needs would be cared for, but I worried about Lee growing up in a single-parent family.

I told Mary that as soon as I returned to Moscow, I'd start looking for a "real" neutral country, like Sweden or Switzerland—one willing to stand up to Washington. I had already retained a Swiss attorney, Dr. Franz Abt, to research the legal issues involved.

Chapter Twenty

Moscow, Again

Within a month of my return to Moscow from Prague, *U.S. News & World Report* announced that I had committed suicide. I learned of this from my mother, who phoned me in panic.

It was, I believe, the long arm of the CIA at work again. I phoned my KGB contact to ask how I should counter the report. He arranged for a KGB press officer to call a number of Moscow-based international correspondents and deny the report. David Remnick from the *Washington Post* was invited to my *dacha* to see for himself that I was alive and well. Unfortunately, Remnick used the visit to write a sour view of me and my life that was not only negative but deliberately incorrect, misquoting me several times. I don't expect American reporters to love me, but I assumed—till now—that they'd try to get their facts straight.

I've never had good luck with the media. In the summer of 1990, Diane Sawyer of ABC News was in Moscow taping a segment on the new leadership of the KGB. She interviewed General Kryuchkov, and after repeated requests, I agreed to talk to her on camera.

I specified in advance the subjects I was willing to discuss: my present-day life in Moscow; not whether I did or did not tell the Soviets this, that or the other thing. Sawyer's producers and I agreed to a list of questions.

The interview was conducted at the International Trade Center hotel on a warm, sunny day. The cameras clicked on and Sawyer immediately peppered me with "pissing match" questions: Why did you do this? Why did you do that? She didn't ask a single question from our list. I got upset with this stunt and said "Cut!" The interview was over.

Sawyer calmed me down, then asked me about an alleged Swiss bank account. Having told them to stop the camera, I assumed it was off. It wasn't, and the things I then said were used in the finished piece. I then stated that "*if* I had a Swiss account, I certainly would not want it public." It was a cheap, unprofessional trick—the type one might expect from a London tabloid, not ABC News.

After the interview, Sawyer invited me to dinner. What she didn't know was that Mary and Lee had arrived that day in Moscow.

" I'm tired," I said. " I want to go home and make love to my computer."

"What a shame that you have to make love to your computer," said Sawyer. She wanted to take me to an Italian restaurant in Moscow called *Arlekino*.

"I prefer the country," I said. Near my *dacha* is a restaurant called *Archangelskaya*. Sawyer's favorite subject over dinner was the famous people she knew, including Warren Beatty and his sex life. Afterwards, Sawyer insisted on seeing my *dacha*.

Before the interview, I had asked Nik, my KGB contact, to see where the KGB wanted me to take her when she arrived. He contacted Kryuchkov, who said, "Take her anywhere you want."

I called Mary and told her, "Lock the doors, pull the drapes, and don't show yourself." I explained to Sawyer that she couldn't go inside because the house was a mess. She and her producer ran around the yard shooting videotape.

Sawyer broke her interview contract with me, and wound up using footage shot after I had called off the interview. She lied to me and tricked me the same way that other correspondents have lied to me and tried to trick me. I've learned all too well how she and her kind operate. I don't give interviews anymore.

Months passed. Mary and Lee rejoined me for the summer of 1990, and they returned with my parents the following Christmas.

Sasha returned from his two-year stint in Budapest early in 1991 and, to stave off boredom, I asked him to join me on a trip to Georgia. I wanted to return to some of the places I had visited four years before.

What I found were many changes. Instead of the comfortable house we had previously been provided with, we were put into a dreary Intourist hotel with bare rooms and poor service. Tbilisi had become dangerous. Groups of Georgian youths who did not want to serve in the Soviet army roamed the streets with handguns and nothing productive to do. The city was experiencing power and food shortages.

While in Georgia, I phoned Dr. Abt, the Swiss lawyer who had been trying for two years to find me a neutral country. For once he had good news. He told me he had made contact with the Swedish ambassador in Berne, and that I should phone him in a few days from Moscow.

I did so, excitedly. Dr. Abt informed me that the Swedish Ambassador had said that I should make a normal application for immigration, and demonstrate that I had business interests which would support me financially in Sweden.

I translated this into " find a business and then emigrate." I asked Dr. Abt if he could find me a good Swedish lawyer with a background in commerce and immigration. A week later he called me with a name: Jan-Henrik Norden of Stockholm.

Sweden sounded great! It had a long history of acting independently of the policies of the United States. During the Vietnam War, they had willingly harbored American draft evaders.

My next hurdle was to tell the KGB about my plans without upsetting them. I was especially worried that General Kryuchkov might take offense. He had worked hard to make me feel at home and build a new life in Moscow.

I struggled with this question for days, then wrote Kryuchkov a letter. Visiting Sweden would be my first unaccompanied trip outside the Soviet Union since my covert trip to the United States in 1986, and I was worried about how he would interpret this. I told him that my Swiss lawyer thought he had found a way for me to reunite with my family. I assured the General that although I would miss Moscow, I wanted my son to have a good, English-based education. Kryuchkov always respected how important my family was to me, and I hoped he would understand my leaving for this reason.

I wrote Kryuchkov that I would initially scout the legal situation and work with a lawyer to cover myself in the event that the U.S. government became aware of my presence in Sweden and tried to extradite me. Finally, I wrote that I hoped to set up some kind of trade enterprise between the Soviet Union and Sweden and hoped that I could return to Moscow frequently to business.

Kryuchkov's reply was what I expected. The General was only concerned for my security, and he questioned the issue of my safety in Sweden. There was no hint of hurt feelings. He asked me to think about my plans for another week and if, after that, I still wished to proceed, I was free to leave.

I complied with his wishes, and in late February, I informed Sasha that I would depart for Sweden in two weeks. Sasha relayed my plans to his management. They issued me a multiple-entry visa for my real—Edward Lee Howard—tourist passport. They wished me good luck and told me to catch the first plane home if things didn't work out.

This first trip to Sweden required stealth, as I still did not know the Swedish position with regard to extradition arrangements with the United States. For this kind of information, I needed to consult with Jan-Henrik Norden in Stockholm.

To cover my tracks, I told my wife and parents over their FBI-bugged phones that I would be visiting Siberia on business for a few weeks. By covert means, I passed word that I would actually be in Sweden, working on relocation issues.

And so I flew to Sweden in mid-March on a regularly-scheduled SAS flight from Moscow to Stockholm, using my U.S. tourist passport. I easily cleared Customs and Immigration, and I took the airport shuttle to a downtown hotel.

I was tense. Had the CIA gotten wind of my travel plans? Would they be waiting at my hotel? This was my first trip to the West since 1986, and I was traveling under my real name. The manhunt for me in September, 1985 had been extensive, and I didn't exactly know what I could expect from the Swedes. Were they truly neutral? Or would they turn their heads if the CIA conducted a kidnapping operation?

My hotel check-in was normal. No police or security agents watching. I turned on the TV in my room and watched the news. Everyone in Sweden looked healthy and happy, unlike the Muscovites, who looked chronically depressed and vitamin deficient.

Yes, Sweden seemed like the right choice for my family.

I walked the streets of Stockholm in a cheerful mood that evening. For the first time in many years I felt optimistic about my situation. Mary and Lee would love Stockholm, and we could all be together again. Sweden put human rights first and politics second. Or so I thought.

Chapter Twenty-One

Covert Sweden

Stockholm was expensive. Two subway stops on the metro cost two dollars compared with five cents for all-day metro use in Moscow. But I was prepared for any price to be with my family.

I told this to Jan-Henrik Norden at our first meeting, on March 15th, two days after I arrived in Sweden.

I asked about lawyer-client confidentiality in Sweden. It is privileged, like in the United States. So I offered an hour-long explanation of who I was and what I wanted, using newspaper articles and the David Wise book to illustrate my situation.

Jan-Henrik was absorbed by my story. He asked questions, particularly about my legal status in the Soviet Union, about the CIA's charges against me, about my probation problem in New Mexico.

We agreed to meet the following Tuesday. Jan-Henrik asked how he could contact me and I told him where I was staying, using my old alias "Scott Roth." Jan-Henrik frowned. I assured him I was in Sweden legally, and showed him the immigration stamp in my Edward Lee Howard passport.

I wrote Mary a positive letter, describing Stockholm and suggesting that she consider a trip to Stockholm within the next month to evaluate the city for herself.

On my return to Jan-Henrik's office, he asked many more questions concerning my flight from the United States and about my probation case in New Mexico. He had found a copy of David Wise's book in Swedish, and had phoned Dr. Abt in Switzerland to discuss my case. He concluded that his chief task would be to research the legality of my extradition from Sweden based upon charges that might be presented by the Americans. I agreed, adding that I also wanted him to prepare a case made for my permanent immigration to Sweden.

"First things first," he said. "The most important thing is to keep you out of jail in case the Americans present the Swedish government a warrant for your arrest."

Jan-Henrik said he would have to research the extradition process himself to avoid bandying my name about. This would not be cheap. I paid him a retainer.

We met once a week for the next six weeks. I found an efficiency apartment near the city center and rented it in the name of Scott Roth. I spent a month doing the museum circuit and sightseeing.

Mary flew over at the end of April and stayed a week. We planned to meet again in Moscow for the summer.

To get a better picture of my probation violation charge, Jan-Henrik contacted Mortin Simon, my lawyer in Santa Fe. Jan-Henrik was becoming convinced that Swedish law would not allow extradition. Espionage—or alleged espionage—is generally considered a political act in Sweden, not a crime, and thereby not extraditable. Jan-Henrik's report was ready the first week of May. In a nutshell, he was ninety percent certain that I could not be extradited from Sweden for either alleged espionage or probation violation. The latter was not as clear-cut as the former, but two factors benefited my position. One, no one had been physically harmed in the assault for which I was given probation; two, seven years had elapsed since the crime was committed.

But at a probably ninety-percent success rating, things were looking good. The next step was emigration.

Jan-Henrik said I would need a business reason for living there. After two years of Swedish residence on a business visa, I would be eligible for permanent resident status. That was the essence of his advice: "Get a business going here."

Anticipating this, I had conceived plans to start a consulting enterprise for trade between Sweden and the Soviet Union. I certainly had the right credentials: business management experience, fluent Russian, and a multiple entry visa for the U.S.S.R. Jan-Henrik liked this, and he asked me to write a business plan for submission along with a business visa application. This would have to be done through the Swedish consulate in Moscow. So in early May I caught an SAS flight home.

Jan-Henrik's meticulous research would soon be put to the test.

Chapter Twenty-Two

Putsch in Moscow

Summer at my dacha is always a delight. Muscovites consider Zhukovka a prized summer destination. It is near the Moscow River and abounds with trees.

The day after my arrival home, Sasha and Nik met me at my villa for coffee.

"How did it go there?" asked Sasha. "Were you threatened? Does it look like you can stay there? Can the Americans get you extradited from there?"

I briefed them on what Jan-Henrik had said. They were skeptical about his analysis, but said they would introduce me to officials from the Moscow Chamber of Commerce who would supply me with ideas and business contacts.

I called Mary at her FBI-tapped home telephone to tell her I'd returned from "Siberia."

A month later, she and Lee arrived for a lazy summer together at the *dacha*. I met with the Moscow Chamber of Commerce and commercial organizations, researching a Swedish business plan. I also visited the Swedish consulate for their guidance on my business plan.

My former neighbor, Boris Yeltsin, was elected President of Russia. My friends and neighbors constantly debated the proposed economic reforms. The prices of basic commodities—bread, milk, etc.—took priority over all other subjects. After prices, the next topic discussed was the short supply of consumer goods.

Russia was in full-blown economic crisis in the summer of 1991; its politicians locked in a power struggle over economic reforms. The Communists accused the reformers of "selling out" to the West. Some saw free enterprise and private ownership as the way to earn more money and be free of the state. Others wanted the state to arrest the "speculators" who were selling goods at higher prices and to restore and preserve the way of life they had come to expect after seventy years of communism.

I attempted to stay out of these debates. My friends knew I believed in private business and less government control. But I did not believe it was my place as a "guest" in the Soviet Union to voice my opinion. I also had my self-preservation in mind.

I finished my business plan in July. The capital for getting started would come from the funds the KGB had given me for resettlement. But it wouldn't last long and Sweden was expensive. I did not, therefore, have the luxury of time, but needed to generate a profit almost immediately.

On August 4, 1991, I submitted my business plan with visa application to the Swedish consulate, and sent copies of everything to Jan-Henrik, for follow-up in Stockholm.

Two weeks later, on August 19, Moscow went crazy. I first got wind of something happening as I stood on the balcony of my *dacha*, my first cup of coffee my hand.

"Ed!" my guard shouted up at me. "There's been a coup in the government!" His ear was all but glued to a small transistor radio.

With Mikhail Gorbachev "ill" in his *dacha* on the southern coast, an eight-member council called the "State Committee for the State of Emergency" had been assembled to take over the government. The junta was headed by Vice President Gennady Yanayev and included Prime Minister Valentin Pavlov, Defense Minister Dimitri Yazov, Minister of the

Interior Boris Pugo, and my old friend, KGB Chairman Vladimir Kryuchkov.

Mary and I switched on the TV. At noon, an army patrol appeared and six soldiers camped outside my *dacha* gates. My neighbor said they were sent to protect the many government *dacha*s in Zhukovka.

Tanks rolled into Moscow. Russians filled the squares and streets in front of the Parliament Building, the "Russian White House."

We had planned to drive into the city for dinner at George Blake's apartment. We departed at 5 p.m., but found the streets clogged and cars being turned back. We gave up. I stopped at the nearby Hotel Ukraine to phone Blake and asked him to give us rain check.

When I came out of the hotel, I was amazed to see Lee, eight years old, standing up on a tank, talking to the soldiers inside! I joined him and found that the tank drivers were young men with little idea about why they were there or what they were supposed to do. A quarter mile away, Boris Yeltsin also stood on a tank, condemning the coup as illegal, insisting that Gorbachev be returned to office, and calling on local officials to disobey the orders of the coup leaders. It was his finest hour.

Next morning I learned from my guards that Yeltsin had escaped captivity in his *dacha* by only a few minutes.

"Some of our people went to pick up Yeltsin yesterday morning when the coup was announced," a guard told me. "But he got the word and left his place twenty minutes before we arrived. Someone must have advised him."

Sasha called me and said excursions into town would not be wise except for emergencies. A lot of alcohol flowed in downtown Moscow that night, and things got out of control. My friends told me that the people with the most to lose—the young, new businessmen and reformers—gave food, vodka and cognac to the young soldiers and tank commanders. This was a clever ploy to keep the soldiers from turning on the crowds in the event they were ordered to shoot. It is not in a Russian's nature to accept hospitality from someone one moment and then, five minutes later, open fire on them.

The tide turned when certain army units began to support Yeltsin and vowed to protect Parliament. There were reports that junta members—notably Yanayev and Pavlov—had left their posts and were drinking in their *dacha*s or apartments. One rumor, which I discounted, was that Kryuchkov ordered his crack Alpha Unit troops to storm the Parliament building and they had refused.

Within two days, it was clear that the army would not fight against the people—and it was the majority of those people in the streets who backed Yeltsin. I kept asking myself, where were the fifteen million members of the Communist Party?

On August 22, Kryuchkov and Yazov flew to Gorbachev's *dacha* to turn themselves in. The putsch leaders were arrested, but ultimately granted amnesty. General Kryuchkov was put in jail, leaving me to contemplate my fate.

Chapter Twenty-Three

After the Fall

At his trial, General Kryuchkov testified that Mikhail Gorbachev knew about the putsch plans in advance and condoned them. My friends inside the KGB also maintain that Gorbachev knew and approved the putsch. They also dispute Gorbachev's contention that his communications with Moscow were cut off during the putsch. Gorbachev's *dacha*, they say, was the Russian equivalent of Camp David and, as such, was equipped to communicate even in the event of nuclear war. Cutting off his independent communication system would have been virtually impossible. My friends say Gorbachev waited to see which side won, and sided with the victor.

Upon returning to Moscow, Gorbachev named General Leonid Shebarshin to take over the KGB. I welcomed this, as I knew Shebarshin and respected him. Shebarshin's tenure was to be short lived, however, when Parliament voiced their displeasure at having a KGB chief with close ties to Kryuchkov. Within a week, they named Vadim Bakatin, a more liberal choice.

Boris Yeltsin soon rose from dissident President of Russia to true leader. When Gorbachev addressed the Russian Parliament on his confinement during the putsch, Yeltsin repeatedly interrupted him on the podium—something unheard of in the history of the Soviet Union. In earlier times, such a person would have been hauled off and shot.

Yeltsin's followers moved to consolidate their new power and popularity. It was soon announced that the KGB would be broken into different departments under different leaders. Yeltsin's intention was to dismantle the power base of the KGB chairman and make the KGB more like security services in the West. In the United States, the CIA handles foreign intelligence, the FBI handles domestic security and the Secret Service guards the President. The former Second Directorate of the KGB was transformed into the Ministry of Security, concentrating on internal security. The former First Directorate became the Russian Central Intelligence Service (the Russian CIA) and would concentrate on foreign intelligence matters. Eugeny Primakov was named to head the Russian CIA. I've never met Primakov, but he was George Blake's supervisor at the Institute of World Economy in Moscow, and Blake spoke well of him.

This massive reorganization and change of leadership had an unsettling effect on the leaders of the KGB. For the first few months, the senior staff stayed in their offices, gossiped about the changes and played games on their computers. They suffered disorientation and low morale.

Talk surfaced about the CIA and Russian Intelligence Service working together to combat terrorism and narcotics trafficking. From mortal enemies to associates overnight! This was mind-boggling to the KGB people I knew. A few KGB officers stationed abroad even jumped ship to the western services during this period of identity crisis. In Stockholm in December, 1991, FBI officers said they were "turning away KGB defectors by the boatload."

My attitude toward all this was one of personal detachment. My only connection with the CIS government is my *dacha*, which they own. I was concerned for my friends and where they might land. It was hard for me to watch them despair for their careers.

The KGB was just a microcosm of what was going on throughout the country. Millions of people who worked for the state awoke to find the Communist Party gone and that they were now personally responsible for their own futures, a concept previously unheard of. No longer could they depend on the state to care for them from cradle to grave. No longer could they turn to the writings of Lenin to help them solve their problems. Virtually everything they had been taught to believe about life for more than seventy years had been discarded overnight.

Parents wondered how they would explain to their children that a year ago Lenin was always right about everything and now he was wrong. As food prices skyrocketed, pensioners worried about how they would feed themselves in a state that no longer felt an obligation to care for them after years of service.

The black marketeers, a small segment of the population, were best prepared to prosper from a new system based on money instead of party privilege.

These people had been at the bottom of Soviet society. They were streetwise, with little formal education. They quickly moved into the hoarding of food supplies, the controlling of alcohol distribution and the buying up of natural resources. Turning a quick ruble was the name of the game.

The Russian mafia consolidated their power, unafraid of the splintering KGB. Before, they had operated in the shadows. Now they came into the open. Their operations multiplied.

When I first arrived in Moscow, its streets were safe. Today we go around at night with mace in our pockets and alarm systems in our cars.

I expected to move to Sweden at the end of October, 1991. By late September I hadn't heard about the visa and I contacted the Swedish consulate. They were of little help, but Jan-Henrik found out that my business plan was being reviewed by a business professor at a small university in the northern part of Sweden.

My patience had worn thin by November. Against Jan-Henrik's advice, I made another quiet visit to Stockholm and found a small house in a northern suburb of Stockholm near a British school. Jan-Henrik received a fax from the Swedish Immigration Board. It was positive. A "real" neutral country had approved my immigration request, and the entire process was done in my own name, and without help from the KGB or the Soviet government.

Chapter Twenty-Four

Trouble Comes Calling

I returned to Moscow to collect my visa and to arrange shipment of my household goods to Stockholm. On December 18, 1991, I arrived back in Sweden as an officially-approved resident. No more fake passports or assumed names.

Next morning, I returned to await Mary and Lee's flight from the States. A blond man with a mustache seemed out of place. Then I was paged. A phone call. It was Jan-Henrik's wife to say she had a call at 3 a.m. from Mary. Mary had missed her flight, due in any minute, and would arrive instead on Finnair from Helsinki, an hour later.

I wandered upstairs to the airport cafeteria for breakfast. When I returned to international arrivals, the blond man was still waiting. Was he also waiting for someone from New York who had been delayed? Not bloody likely.

Alarm bells rang in my head, but I calmed myself. "He probably works here," I reasoned.

Mary and Lee exited the customs gate and we all hugged each other. For the first time in six years, we were meeting in a free country and we were on the road to permanent reunification. They were tired and happy. I was ecstatic.

A taxi drove us to the small house I'd rented in Enebyberg, a suburb north of Stockholm. We relaxed, settled in and readied ourselves for the holidays.

We decorated the house for Christmas, unpacked my things from Moscow and explored Stockholm.

Two days after Christmas, about 8:30 a.m., there was a knock on the door. I opened it. Two men flashed police badges.

"Are you Edward Howard?" one of them asked.

I told them that I was. I showed them into the kitchen and excused myself to change from nightclothes into something more suitable. I told Mary two policemen were in the kitchen and she thought I was joking.

I offered the policemen coffee but they declined. The senior man was Inspector Foresburg who, I later discovered, ran the Soviet section of the Swedish Security Police.

"We know who you are and have to inform you that there are some FBI officers in town who wish to speak with you," said Foresburg. "We have nothing against you but request that you talk to them. You may do so in our presence if you wish." Foresburg added that it was their duty to protect me since I was here legally and had the right to remain in Sweden as a tourist for up to ninety days.

"I am not here as a tourist," I told them. "I am here on a business immigration visa to work and live here and the visa is valid for six months."

They were surprised by this; they asked to see my passport and visa.

"Nevertheless, the FBI officers would still like to talk with you," said Foresburg. "Can we tell them to come here? One says that he knows Mrs. Howard."

"Where are they?" I asked.

"About five minutes away by car. We can call them on the mobile phone. They very much want to talk with you."

"I'll bet they do," I said. "The answer is no and I want to call my lawyer now right now."

I phoned Jan-Henrik at home, told him the situation, and handed the phone to Foresburg. They spoke. Foresburg handed the phone back to me. Jan-Henrik told me not to meet with the FBI without him. Accordingly, I informed the Security Police officers I would not meet the FBI that day and that all future communications should be through my lawyer.

As they prepared to leave, Mary asked Inspector Foresburg which FBI officers said they knew her.

"Special Agent Hudenko and Special Agent Nelson. Do you remember them?"

"Yes," said Mary. "One is from New Mexico and the other is from Minnesota,"

The Swedish Police officers departed, with Jan-Henrik's phone number for the FBI. Mary and I both stared silently out the kitchen window at the snow for a couple of minutes.

"They don't give up. Don't they realize this isn't their territory?" I said.

"It's just like the bad dream of Santa Fe, but six years later," said Mary.

I felt confident with Jan-Henrik's legal analysis. Sweden was a neutral country. The FBI couldn't just show up at your door. Or so I thought. Later that morning, as I took out the garbage, a dark blue Volvo 740 with U.S. embassy license plates passed my house then turned around for a second pass. I ran inside to grab my camera, but the car was gone when I returned to the street. I wanted to show the Swedish police that U.S. officers were not keeping their distance.

Jan-Henrik and the FBI officers exchanged several telephone calls. Jan-Henrik proposed that we meet at his office after the New Year's Day, but the FBI wanted to meet at the U.S. embassy before New Year so they could return home to their families in time for the holiday—and with me in custody, they hoped.

We reached a compromise: I agreed to meet the FBI officers on December 30, 1991, at Jan-Henrik's office for one hour. I figured that's all we'd need for them to state their points and for me to reply.

I took the subway into town for the meeting. On the way, I visited an electronics store and purchased a microcassette recorder, which I hid in my suit pocket.

Four FBI officers were waiting in Jan-Henrik's office: John Hudenko and James Shaw of the Albuquerque office, Richard Nelson from the Minneapolis office and John Thierault of the London office. They began the meeting by asking me to sign a statement confirming I had been advised of my rights. Jan-Henrik advised me not to sign so I did not sign.

Next, the FBI advised me that they were proceeding with my prosecution on two charges: alleged espionage-interstate flight and probation violation. They said they were not going to try to arrest me in Sweden, but they strongly urged that I give myself up.

"You have no place to go now except Cuba," said Hudenko. "And we don't think that will be an option for you within two years," This suggested that they believed the KGB was in disarray, and that I was no longer welcome in Moscow.

I said nothing.

Agent Thierault told me that they were going to "make life hell for me" in Sweden. I liked that statement, especially since I was secretly recording this session. What would the Swedes think when they heard that a U.S. government agency was unilaterally taking police actions inside their country?

I baited Thierault to make more statements of this kind, asking if that meant having my son expelled from school in Sweden, as they had done in Hungary.

"Yes," Thierault replied, "if that's what it takes..."

"That wasn't us," Hudenko cut him off. "That was the embassy."

Their message was simple: Make it easy on yourself by coming back now, voluntarily. They said if I didn't, they would do everything possible via all channels to get me out of Sweden. They told me that the KGB was a sunken ship and that they were turning away potential KGB defectors by the boat-load.

My message to them was equally simple: I wanted to live in peace with my family and build a life in Sweden. Sure, I might return to the United States one day, but I would pick the date, not them.

Agent Hudenko, a clever professional, played psychologist and asked me to tell them some of the "great mysteries" in which I had been involved since leaving the U.S.A. He wanted information about what I was doing and how my business was going. I played along, giving him information I knew they already had or could find out easily from the Swedish authorities.

I asked Hudenko about his family name. "You have a Ukrainian name."

"Yes," he said. "Do you know the area?"

"It's a wonderful place," I replied. "I've been there a couple of times. I think they will soon break away from Moscow and secede."

"Do you have inside information on that?" he quickly asked.

I laughed and told him I had no inside information; I was only making a prediction.

The agents gave me their business cards and Hudenko asked if he could have his photo taken with me. He had been on my case for many years and wanted a souvenir of our meeting. His motive was transparent: the FBI wanted a current close-up shot of me for their file. Nonetheless, I agreed, since the Swedes could give them my visa photo if they asked for it.

I announced that their hour was up and that I had another engagement. They were polite about leaving and I shook their hands as they left Jan-Henrik's office.

Jan-Henrik and I discussed the meeting for another thirty minutes. He phoned Inspector Foresburg to report that the meeting had taken place. We both agreed that nothing unusual or unexpected had come from the meeting. They wanted me back and offered nothing.

"What a waste of the taxpayer's money," I said. "They could have sent me a fax through you or Foresburg and accomplished the same thing."

I told Mary not to worry about the FBI, but she knew better. They had done the job once in Hungary, and now they were going to do it again here. I wondered whether Sweden would really defend its neutrality. To harbor and protect hundreds of draft evaders during the Vietnam War was one thing, since most of the American public and most Europeans felt the war was wrong. But to defend the rights of an immigrant accused of espionage was something else. But we hoped for the best. Mary and Lee returned to the U.S.A. in January, as planned. They would apply for Swedish residency permits and return in the summer. Lee would attend the British school; Mary would begin studying Swedish immediately.

Chapter Twenty-Five

More Harassment

My house seemed very empty without my wife and son. I busied myself with registering my business, opening a bank account and cultivating contacts.

I attended a free Swedish language course for immigrants that offered twice-weekly classes at a nearby high school. I swore that it would be the last foreign language I'd have to learn!

My neighbors in Enebyberg were polite but reserved. I suspected it was going to take years to make real friends.

But then I made a contact at a firm downtown called SOVTRADE. I'd seen their name in a telephone book and assumed they had business with the U.S.S.R. Ola Friskopp and Ulla Berstrom welcomed me into their office. Ulla had lived in Moscow for six years and knew Moscow and Russia well. Her husband, Ola, was a marketing specialist with many contacts in the Swedish business world. During the next seven months we developed several business projects together and had fun in Stockholm and Moscow.

The breakup of the Soviet Union was working against us, but in the spring of 1992 the three of us signed three separate contracts to import Russian wood into Sweden. Signing contracts and getting delivery were quite separate matters, it turned out. The first Russian businessman disappeared after signing a contract to deliver 50,000 cubic meters of wood. The second businessman had his wood turned away at the port of Leningrad because the port was "overloaded."

Translation: the port director wanted a bribe of five-dollars-per-cubic-meter. We declined.

The third businessman was Edward Boltov, the director of a Russian company called INFOTECH. INFOTECH dealt primarily with information technology, but had rights from the Russian government to export wood in order to generate hard currency earnings for their information business. SOVTRADE and I negotiated a contract for INFOTECH to deliver 500,000 cubic meters of pine, spruce and birch to Sweden. The wood never materialized and we broke off contact with Boltov after several months of waiting.

Business looked grim, but I resolved to plod on for at least one year.

In April I visited the local police station to renew my residence permit, which expired in mid-May. The officer on duty seemed to know all about me. She knew that my wife had been to the Swedish consulate in the United States to apply for residency.

The officer told me that it "was up to the political powers" to make a judgment about my visa extension. This was a signal that my residency status in Sweden was getting sticky.

Jan-Henrik advised that I not take a planned business trip out of the country until my visa was extended, but I made a trip to Russia.

Back in Moscow, Sasha warned me that the Swedish police planned to arrest me on the day my residence permit expired, May 14.

I was puzzled. Why would the Swedes arrest me? I had done nothing wrong in Sweden. I paid taxes and ran an open and honest business. I had to return and find out what was going on.

Sasha tried to discourage me from returning, but I told him I had too much invested not to return. Mary and I were placing our hopes on Sweden for a life together. There was nowhere else. And what Sasha told me in Moscow just didn't make sense. Why, if they wanted me out of Sweden, didn't they just ask me to leave? Today I know the answer to that question, and it shames the neutrality of Sweden and the integrity of the Swedish police, but I'll get to that.

I returned to Sweden on May 12 to meet my parents, who were to arrive, as fate would have it, on May 14. They arrived. I watched for tails on me; there were none. But I told my parents to expect trouble. Nothing happened that day.

My parents saw the sights and thoroughly enjoyed Stockholm. And they left, not noticing an unusual phenomena that was taking place on my street.

Normally, a truck would appear every Tuesday for garbage removal. But sometime in May, I personally acquired a level of garbage service most people would envy: daily pickup.

Shades of Santa Fe! There was no question, I had been targeted by SAPO—the Swedish Security Police.

Meanwhile, still no word on my visa extension application. Only a lame excuse that my application had to be reviewed by the same professor who reviewed my initial application. Neither Jan-Henrik or I believed this. Mary was waiting for news. And a deposit was required to hold Lee's reservation at the British school.

In late June I had to return to Moscow on business. On my return, I was detained by customs and strip-searched.

Jan-Henrik received word that my case was being handled personally by the Swedish Immigration Board's deputy director, Per-Erik Nilsson, who wished to meet with me to discuss my case. A meeting was scheduled for July 6 at Jan-Henrik's office.

During the one-hour meeting Jan-Henrik presented my case. Nilsson presented us with a secret memo in which the

Swedish Security Police recommended denial of my visa extension on grounds that I was probably working for the KGB, and that I had not reported this on my visa application.

I replied that I was not a KGB agent, nor had been anything but truthful on my application. I had used my real name and my valid U.S. passport. Would the KGB, I pointed out, send a man like me—a man known throughout the Western world as an accused spy—to spy on Sweden? The idea was ludicrous!

Nilsson took notes and promised a fair review of my case. He added that he was reading David Wise's book about me. I could see in his eyes that the game was already over.

On July 24, I faxed Nilsson to ask for his determination, but he never replied. I'd already told Mary to visit Sweden as a tourist. I wanted to have at least a few days with her and Lee before the roof came down on me.

In early August I flew to Moscow on business. Jan-Henrik phoned to say he had received a fax from Nilsson. It was negative on my application. I returned to Stockholm on August 8 to pack my things and tie up loose ends. I wanted only to enjoy a couple of weeks with my family before leaving.

But unbeknownst to me, a classic covert action game was underway, orchestrated by the U.S. government. They'd been cooking the stew for a long time with many ingredients.

Chapter Twenty-Six

Jail Time

Mary, Lee and I were having dinner. We had only a few days left together in Stockholm before they went west and I went east. The telephone rang. It was a local newspaper reporter. He cited a recent story about me from the *Albuquerque Journal* and asked for an interview. I told him "no comment" and referred him to my lawyer.

I hung up and told Mary the press was on the case. Only two weeks to go and someone was stirring the pot.

Jan-Henrik phoned to say the reporter was going to write a story with us or without us, so we'd better get our side of the story on the record. I reluctantly agreed, and met with the reporter at Jan-Henrik's office 10 p.m. that evening.

The reporter and his photographer were anxious to get something for their morning edition. They had a copy of the *Albuquerque Journal* story that reported my presence in Sweden "according to sources in Washington." They also had the David Wise book, and for the next hour and a half walked through who I was, whether I was a KGB spy, and why I was in Sweden.

I answered all of their questions and even addressed the meeting I'd had with FBI officers in Stockholm that previous December. This excited the reporter. I stressed that all I had wanted of Sweden was a place to live with my family, but the government had decided not to approve my residence visa so I was in the process of leaving.

At eight the next morning, there was another invasion of my privacy. This time, a local television station. I declined an interview, and of course the reporter said he'd do the story with me or without me.

Wishing to counter Washington's propaganda, I got dressed and did an interview in the backyard of my house. The reporter was moved by my plight and he gave me some advice as he left.

"This house is going to be swarming with reporters in a couple of hours. If I were you, Mr. Howard, I'd get out of here for a couple of days and take my family to a downtown hotel or to the country."

I sensed he was right, and I moved Mary, Lee and myself to a downtown hotel. When we arrived, I called Jan-Henrik to tell him where we were. We stayed close to the hotel, and at one point I diverted my son's attention from a newsstand, where a photo of me featured prominently.

Jan-Henrik phoned me that evening to say that he had watched my television interview and that he felt I'd given a favorable impression of myself. He said that a Swedish member of parliament was questioning publicly why FBI officers had been allowed to interview me in Sweden without Swedish police officers present.

The next day, I scouted my house for reporters and found none, so we returned home. The day after that, I went downtown, with Mary and Lee, to tie up some business matters. As we crossed a street, a Volvo pulled up on the curb. Two young men jumped out and flashed their badges at me.

"Mr. Howard, please come with us. We have to take you in for questioning."

I was startled. I hardly had time to say goodbye to Mary and Lee. I asked Mary to phone Jan-Henrik.

During our short ride to Stockholm city jail, I asked the officers if it had been their man I had seen following me in a red car earlier that day.

"No, we are trying to keep him away from you," they said. "He's a photographer."

The Swedish police didn't like that I was taking my case to the media. They feared that public opinion, usually quite liberal in Scandinavia, would weigh against Swedish cooperation with Washington. In jail I would look like a criminal, not an average, ordinary family man doing interviews in a quiet garden.

On signing their arrest document, I was asked, incongruously, if I wanted the assistance of a U.S. consular officer.

"You must be joking," I told them. "If it weren't for the U.S. embassy, I wouldn't be here today."

They all laughed. They said that I was being charged with overstaying my visa, and that they would notify my attorney.

The arrest warrant had been signed by none other than the back-stabbing bureaucrat, Per-Erik Nilsson himself. In my July 6 meeting with him, we all entered into a "gentlemen's agreement" that if my request for an extension was denied, I would be granted adequate time to pack my bags and leave. Instead, Nilsson chose to have me arrested on the street, without notice.

The police escorted me to a private prison cell, luxurious by international standards. It was a room approximately seven-by-fourteen feet and it was furnished with a bed, a wash basin and a desk. The food was bland, but they served chocolate cake on Sunday. My jailers brought me English-language paperbacks and, within a day, provided me with a radio.

I was almost totally cut off from the world and the events surrounding my case. I listened to the radio broadcasts but

I didn't understand enough Swedish to fully comprehend what they said about me. My only contacts with the outside world were Jan-Henrik's visits and a once-a-day call to Mary.

On the night I was arrested, the Swedish Security Police conducted a thorough search of my house, looking for drugs or spy paraphernalia. They used mirrors to check behind boards, and they took all my books, my computer and many other things.

"It was just like the FBI in Santa Fe seven years ago, Ed," Mary later told me. I was very concerned about how this ordeal was affecting my son.

Jan-Henrik called me in the morning, after my first night in jail, to say the Security Police wanted a meeting us that afternoon.

Two SAPO officers announced that I was being charged with violating sections 19:5 and 19:10 of the Swedish Criminal Code: espionage for a foreign power. I was floored!

The Swedish Security Police took a great interest in my contract with INFOTECH, believing that the Russians were keen on stealing Swedish technology. Of course, I had dealt with INFOTECH because of their license to export wood.

We adjourned to another room for questioning. The SAPO officers announced that the session would be tape-recorded, and they repeated that I was being charged and investigated for espionage against Sweden.

My first response was anger. I told them that this whole affair was something out of a Franz Kafka novel; that there was no basis whatsoever for the charges, and no evidence had been offered. I agreed to freely answer their questions on one condition: that my answers would be for SAPO use only and would not be given to any foreign power.

The senior SAPO officer bristled at my request, saying he had no plans to turn anything over to anyone. He agreed to my request.

SAPO asked me straight questions and I gave straight answers. I knew that the Swedes had no evidence of any espionage; they were simply on a fishing expedition.

My second interrogation, the following day, focused on what I did in the Soviet Union after my arrival, what my sources of income were, and what I did while I was in Moscow on business trips. It was clear to me what was going on. Few of these questions related to alleged spying in Sweden, but all of them smacked of the FBI. Nonetheless, I cooperated and told them the truth about my arrival in the Soviet Union in 1985.

SAPO asked me if I had ever contacted the KGB before September of 1985, and I denied this FBI allegation. I told them I had been in Hungary and Czechoslovakia on false passports because that's what I had been given to use by the authorities in each case. I told them of my work as an economic consultant in Moscow and denied ever having joined the KGB or Communist Party. I also told them about the funds I had received for resettlement purposes from the Soviet government and about my *dacha* and apartment in Moscow. Everything I told them was the truth. I had nothing to hide; I was in Sweden as a private businessman trying to build a new life.

Toward the end of this session, I asked them if they had any questions about my activities in Sweden, rather than places outside their jurisdiction. Except for the issue of my trade contracts in Sweden, they had none. This left no doubt in my mind: the entire affair was a set-up by the FBI.

Jan-Henrik and I had a chance to discuss my case privately. We were upbeat. My legitimate business in Sweden was well documented. My actions in other countries, though

perhaps of interest to SAPO, had no bearing on the espionage charges made against me in Sweden. We knew that
SAPO was relaying the results of my interrogation to the
Swedish prosecutor by name of K.G. Swenson, who had
built a reputation for himself in espionage cases. He felt that
Swenson was controlling many of the questions put to me
by SAPO. If that was the case, I asked, why are we not being
asked questions about espionage activities in Sweden? By
this time, even Jan-Henrik realized that the line of questioning was odd.

The third and final day of my interrogation, SAPO announced that they had run a legal tap on my home phone
since April. They questioned me about everything I had said
for months over the phone. Who were my Russian trade
contacts? Who was the woman I identified as my marketing
representative there? Did we have an amorous relationship?
Why was I teaching English to some people in Moscow? I
calmly gave them the simple answers to their questions. The
SAPO officers shook my hand and told me they would
present their findings to the prosecutor the next day.

Jan-Henrik called SAPO and reported back to me that their
mood was relaxed and cheerful. "Why?" I thought. They
didn't break me down or prove their case. They didn't meet
their objective. Unless their real objective was to find out
everything I'd been doing the past several years for the FBI.

This thought angered me and I asked Jan-Henrik if I could
bring suit for false arrest. He said that such suits were very
difficult to win, and advised me to concentrate on getting
out of jail and fighting for my continued residence in Sweden. I reluctantly agreed.

The next day, Monday, I tried to engross myself in a
French romance novel. By noon I heard the good news from
Jan-Henrik: the espionage charges were being dropped. The
bad news was that I was to remain in jail as a "security risk"

until the government decided whether to deport me or let me reside in Sweden. Here I was, having lived in Sweden for eight months, under wire-tap and surveillance, having undergone interrogation, having been found completely and utterly clean and the Swedes still wanted to hold me in jail!

Before Sweden would make their decision, I needed to make mine—did I want to stay or leave?

I knew I would stay in jail until Thursday when the Prime Minister and his cabinet met and considered my case and my request to continue living in Sweden. I also knew I could leave and go back to Moscow and continue my life there without my family. I had fought to live together with them for seven years, and this was probably my last chance. Yet I also knew that Prime Minister Bildt was chummy with the CIA and no friend of mine. I felt sure that his government would say no to my continued residence in Sweden.

To continue my battle to live in Sweden, I would practically have to seek political asylum before the courts. To achieve this, I would have to demonstrate that my life in Russia was intolerable and dangerous. This was certainly not the case and I did not want to offend my Russian friends and hosts by claiming that their hospitality had threatened me.

The major problem of returning to Moscow would be the loss of my family. I would miss them and they would miss me, but I was only a part of their lives. My son, Lee, had a good school, friends, relatives, and activities that he enjoyed in America. Was it really fair of me to keep pulling them into a messy situation everywhere I went? Maybe it was time to give them a break and make do with summer and Christmas visits? It was better than not seeing them at all, and at least I would know they were leading normal lives in the United States.

After much anguish, I reached a decision: I would withdraw my application for residence in Sweden. This would avoid deportation hearings, stop the scandal in the press, and allow me and my family to get on with our lives, albeit separately.

The next morning I asked for the SAPO officers to come see me. Two hours later an officer arrived. I told him of my decision to leave Sweden as soon as possible. He was startled, but was obviously pleased as he ran off to confer with his boss.

"There's an SAS direct flight to Moscow at 1:30 every afternoon," I yelled at him as he ran down the jail corridor.

Within the hour, Robert reappeared with Jan-Henrik and Jorgen Almblad, the chief of SAPO. They had booked me on the 1:30 flight to Moscow, and now it was a race to get me out of jail, home to pack a bag or two and off to the airport for my flight.

I rode with Jan-Henrik and Jorgen Almblad to the Immigration authority, and Jan-Henrik officially delivered my request to leave Sweden and fly directly to Moscow. I insisted that Jan-Henrik write in a guarantee that I would be flown "directly to Moscow," in case anyone was thinking of flying me elsewhere, into the hands of the FBI.

Jan-Henrik remained at the Immigration office to complete the paperwork while SAPO took me on a high-speed ride to my house in Enebyberg. I phoned Mary on the police car's mobile phone, asking her to pack two bags of clothes for me. She and Lee were waiting for me. I changed into a business suit and added a few more items to my bags. I took five minutes to chat with Lee, and gave him the letter proving my innocence of the spy charges from the Swedish prosecutor.

"You keep this letter," I told him. "This was a big mess but I've been completely cleared. I'll explain more when you and Mom come to Moscow for a visit, and I hope that will be in a few days." Mary and Lee couldn't travel with me that day because they first needed visas from the Russian consulate. I told Mary to follow me as soon as possible and we could spend some quiet time together at my *dacha*.

The SAPO officer said we were running late. "We're going to have to move fast if you are going to make that flight, so put your seat belts on tight."

The normal taxi drive from my house to the airport was forty minutes. The SAPO car made it in under twenty, sirens and lights flashing. Lee loved it, of course, but Mary was worried about the speed and I was worried about missing the flight.

Jan-Henrik and Jorgen Almblad met us at the airport and we drove directly to the plane on the tarmac. Later, I learned why the Swedes had been so anxious to get me out of town: as my plane took off, several FBI officers—including my nemesis, Special Agent John Hudenko—were touching down at the same airport.

Mary met with them the next day, and they told her to tell me they were "sure they'd be seeing me soon."

As I sat down in my seat, the flight attendant gave me a friendly smile and handed me a copy of the *Svenska Dagblatt* with my story and picture on the cover. SAPO had booked me into first- class, but I couldn't relax and enjoy the service until we were over Russian airspace one hour after takeoff.

No one greeted me at the Moscow airport. I called my *dacha* caretaker, Vasil Vasilavitch and asked him for a ride home. He was surprised to hear my voice. The Russian newspapers had been following my plight and my friend was not sure I'd ever be able to come home.

At the *dacha* I phoned Sasha.

"Where are you?" he asked, thinking I was calling from jail.

"Home in my *dacha*," I said. "And I'll be here for a long time."

Mary and Lee arrived the following Friday. After a wasted summer and a traumatic week of imprisonment, we had five days together in peace. We discussed the future. We knew we'd be living separate lives, but we were not going to lose each other—just live apart for most of the year. My decision to throw in the towel and separate was a hard one, but after trying to set up housekeeping in three countries, it was time to let my family get on with their lives. I had fought hard to keep us together, but I had lost.

We had tried to live together as a family in Hungary, Czechoslovakia and Sweden and had been unsuccessful, due to the actions of the United States government. Hungary sold us out for American aid, Czechoslovakia had a velvet revolution and Sweden had a prime minister who was cozy with the CIA. In all cases, I wasn't worth defending. As a resident and taxpayer, my contribution to each country was minimal compared to the diplomatic pressures they had to face from the United States. Only the Soviet Union, now Russia, had shown a genuine caring for me.

I take a small pleasure in occasionally re-reading the angry press release issued by the U.S. Department of Justice the day I left Sweden. It stated that "The Department of Justice position is unyielding: to bring Howard to trial no matter how long it may take, for he will be unable to find a lasting refuge in even in the most remote corners of the earth."

For all they have tried over the years, the American government has only succeeded in forcing me back to a comfortable life in Moscow, that grand, old cultured city of ten million souls. I enjoy my *dacha* in the country, my spacious apartment in the city; I drive a Volvo station wagon, run a profitable business, live a civilized life full of friends and colleagues, and enjoy regular visits from my parents, wife and son. My life isn't perfect, but I get by.

What has the FBI achieved after chasing me around Europe for nine years and spending God knows how many millions of taxpayer dollars? They've got my Moscow address, my fax number and a Kodacolor snapshot of me with John Hudenko.

Chapter Twenty-Seven

Yurchenko, Howard, Ames, Pelton & Company

If Vitaly Yurchenko, a Soviet KGB officer, had not defected to the United States on August 1, 1985, I'd still be enjoying mesquite barbecues at my suburban ranch home in Santa Fe. His actions caused my world crumble around me, and I was forced to flee to Russia to save myself from the CIA and FBI. Now, substituting birch for mesquite, I do my *shashliks* (barbecues) at my *dacha* in Zhukovka.

Inside the KGB, Yurchenko was known as an officer who rose through the ranks on the coattails of his political sponsor on the Central Committee, not for his brilliance as an operations officer. He was not, as the Western press erroneously reported, the "number four man in the KGB." Even before his defection he was not well-liked within his own intelligence agency, and afterwards, he was lucky that his boss, General Kryuchkov, did not order him shot.

At the time of his defection, Yurchenko held the rank of Colonel in the KGB. He served as the deputy chief of the First Department (foreign clandestine operations), and was responsible for operations against the United States. On July 24, 1985, Yurchenko was in Rome to prevent defections among a group of Soviet scientists scheduled to attend a conference in Italy the following month. He told his KGB colleagues he was going to visit a Vatican museum, then disappeared. On August 1, he walked into the U.S. embassy in Rome, asked for political asylum and was immediately flown to the United States. He was taken to a safe house near CIA headquarters, and his debriefing began almost immediately.

Defectors come in every shape and size; they are rated by two yardsticks: their information value and their propaganda value. The country to which he defects must quickly establish whether or not he is a genuine defector (or a double agent, still working for the enemy), and, if genuine, determine his motivation, his value, and his price. Whether or not Yurchenko was a double agent, planted by the KGB to embarrass the United States or to draw fire from their senior mole, Aldrich Ames, remains a mystery.

Yurchenko was classed as a high-level defector. As such, he was debriefed by a joint team of the FBI and CIA's top officers. One team member was Aldrich Hazen ("Rick") Ames, a senior counterintelligence officer in the CIA's Soviet division.

What did Yurchenko know? He would have known the names of U.S. agents already recruited (such as Pelton and Ames), and probably the names of U.S. targets not yet recruited (such as myself).

In the target identification and development process, the KGB or CIA intelligence officer compiles lists of potential agents he'd like to recruit. The next step is to run a name trace on the target and pull up any available records. After that, the agency might investigate their lifestyle, looking for sexual or moral indiscretions which could be used to blackmail the target; or financial excesses, which might indicate that he could be bought.

In the United States, likely KGB targets include employees of U.S. intelligence agencies, staff members of the House and Senate, defense contractor employees, military officers in Washington and the like. Once a target is recruited, the list of people who have access to this information is tightly controlled, whether inside the CIA or KGB.

I learned that the CIA would even resort to using internal disinformation to protect high-level information about agent recruitment from their own employees. The case that sticks in my mind came from my training at Langley. The chief of a European station cabled headquarters to say that recruitment of a certain target was not going to be attempted. A second, " eyes only" cable to the division chief reported just the opposite: that the target had been successfully recruited! The purpose of this spy dance was to give the lower-level employees the idea that the target had been abandoned. The CIA did not even trust its own staff!

Yurchenko revealed the descriptions of two alleged moles inside the American intelligence community. The first was an employee of the National Security Agency (NSA) who had walked through the front door of the Soviet embassy in 1980. He possessed U.S. naval communications secrets to sell, he said, and Yurchenko gave the debriefers his physical description and an approximate description of where he lived. The "walk-in" turned out to be Ronald W. Pelton, who was arrested for espionage on in 1985, convicted and sent to prison for life.

The next mole that Yurchenko described was a man he knew by the code name " Robert." He described Robert as a disgruntled, former CIA employee who had been prepared for assignment to Moscow but whose assignment had been canceled at the last minute. Yurchenko admitted that he had never met "Robert" and didn't know his physical description or real name—just his CIA work history and that he was not happy with the Agency when they terminated him.

According to Ronald Kessler, who interviewed Yurchenko in Russia and wrote a book about the affair, the CIA exercised gross negligence and treated Yurchenko with incredible insensitivity during his three months in the United States. After agreeing to his request for no publicity (similar to the one I made with the KGB after my arrival in Moscow), CIA Director William Casey boasted about Yurchenko's defection throughout Washington and made no effort to keep this secret from the newspapers. For three months the CIA confined Yurchenko to a safe house near Fredericksburg, Virginia, where he was practically imprisoned. On November 2, 1985, a guard named Thomas Hannah took pity on Yurchenko and took him out to a Georgetown bistro for dinner. Yurchenko excused himself to go to the men's room, walked out of the restaurant and over to the Soviet embassy.

The next day, Yurchenko claimed at a press conference to have been drugged and kidnapped by the Americans, who held him against his will until he escaped. When asked about me, Yurchenko said that he did not know me and that the first time he even heard of Edward Howard was when he saw press reports about me. He returned to Moscow soon thereafter, and little has been heard of him since.

How could Yurchenko, a senior KGB defector, go home and expect to escape the firing squad?

General Kryuchkov was incensed about Yurchenko's defection, but Yurchenko's prospects weren't as bleak as some might think. Although General Kryuchkov would have liked to see Yurchenko tried for treason and shot, he had to respect the propaganda value of Yurchenko's re-defection, which gave CIA public relations a black eye.

All of the above notwithstanding, KGB directors have been known to dispense with the niceties and have turncoats shot. A reliable KGB source also told me that Yurchenko saved his neck by convincing Valery Martinov, a KGB officer who had been recruited by the FBI, to return on the same plane with him to Moscow. I was told that Yurchenko showed Martinov his own pardon from Kryuchkov. Martinov believed Yurchenko's pitch and returned to Moscow. Much to his horror, Martinov found that Yurchenko's pardon was limited only to him, and Martinov's so-called "pardon" was a ruse to lure him home.

What must have gone through the minds of the CIA and FBI as they watched both Yurchenko, their public asset, and Martinov, their secret asset, leave Dulles Airport that November day in 1985? On their return, Yurchenko was demoted and transferred to the KGB equivalent of the motor pool. Martinov was executed.

Aldrich ("Rick") Hazen Ames was arrested for espionage with his Colombian-born second wife, Maria del Rosario Casas Dupuy, in February 1994. According to charges contained in a 35-page FBI affidavit, Ames accepted at least $2.7 million for selling his secrets. The FBI alleged that Ames began peddling classified information to the KGB in the spring of 1985, several months before the defection of Vitaly Yurchenko.

Ames, the son of a career CIA man, was an operations officer in the clandestine service. He ran spies. While working in Mexico City in 1982, he recruited his future wife, Maria, a cultural attache at the Colombian embassy. She became a CIA informant, and soon, his lover.

After special training in counterintelligence, Ames was assigned to recruit employees of the Soviet embassy in the spring of 1984. No doubt, he then made valuable contacts among them, which he exploited handsomely later. His first marriage ended in divorce on August 1, 1985; he married Maria nine days later. Shortly thereafter, he returned to Washington and was promoted to chief of the Soviet counterintelligence branch in the SE (Soviet/East European) division. Although his office was directly across the hall from the U.S.S.R. desk where I worked at Langley, I never met Ames.

The FBI alleged that Ames began spying for Moscow in 1985. By May 1985, Ames was banking KGB money. The CIA never paid serious attention to Ames's high living and enormous cash flow.

His huge cash reserves came to light only when the Dominion Bank of Virginia filed reports with the Internal Revenue Service in the late 1980s and early 1990s that Ames was "structuring" his deposits to keep them under $10,000 each, the threshold which requires banks to report deposits of $10,000 or more to the IRS.

Ames pleaded guilty to espionage on April 28, 1994. He was sentenced to life in prison without hope of parole and is currently undergoing extensive damage-assessment debriefing by the FBI and the CIA in a deal to obtain his wife's early release from prison.

Ames and his wife were not ideologues, and they were not seeking revenge. They had a single motive for their spy work: greed. Ames bought a house for $540,000 in cash, ran up to $5,000 a month in credit card bills, spent nearly $100,000 on home improvements and bought a $40,000 red Jaguar XJ-6, which he drove to work—all on a CIA employee's civil service salary of $69,843 a year.

In the words of one intelligence writer, "Ames could not have been positioned to do more damage. As a member of the CIA's Directorate for Operations, he was part of the small, elite element of American intelligence which conducts classical espionage: spying and counterspying with other human agents. For the KGB, it doesn't get any better than this. Ames could supply the details on every agent, operation, technique, and technical gadget. Most important, he could provide feedback to Moscow on how well the U.S. was doing on finding the Soviet/Russian theft of American secrets. For the KGB, Ames may prove to have been the crown jewel in their long streak of Cold War espionage successes."

My friends in the KGB knew Ames was in trouble months before his arrest. They wanted to bring him to Moscow and could have done so. Ames could have driven to Canada or flown to Mexico, where he would have been issued a Russian diplomatic passport; or Ames could have boarded an outbound Russian freighter disguised as a merchant marine.

This plan was shot down by higher authorities due to political considerations. An Ames presence in Moscow, it was thought, would severely disrupt U.S. aid packages to the Commonwealth of Independent States.

Before Ames, the CIA pinned the loss of every American and Russian agent in Moscow on me. Now, Ames has been held responsible for the death of twelve agents, and Vincent Cannistraro, who retired from the CIA in 1990, said, "Ames's disclosures led directly to the killings of two well-placed agents whose unmasking had previously been blamed on a 1985 defector, Edward Lee Howard."

In March of 1994, an Associated Press article on Yurchenko quoted CIA Director Robert Gates as saying the CIA "discovered some problems that couldn't be blamed on Howard." By the time they finish debriefing Ames, the only thing the FBI will be able to charge me with is selling plans of the men's room at Langley.

But one nagging question remains: What motive did Yurchenko have for giving the FBI the description of a mole, "Robert," who perfectly matched my characteristics, if I wasn't that mole?

My answer is this: Yurchenko was using the information they had about "Robert" as "chaff." In military parlance, chaff is an electronic decoy used in warfare by planes or missiles to fool enemy radar. It can be as simple as aluminum foil strips dropped from a plane to sophisticated electronic countermeasures, designed to make enemy radar systems misinterpret the real position of the plane. The radar then directs fire at the chaff, saving the plane. In my case, Ames and other Soviet moles were the plane, and I was the chaff, at whom the CIA and FBI did their firing for six years.

As deputy chief of the American Department, Yurchenko was in the right position to know my target profile. From my diplomatic passport and visa application they knew that Edward Lee Howard was to have been posted to the U.S. embassy in Moscow as second secretary. They also knew that my assignment had been canceled at the last minute. The KGB knew that I had called the U.S. embassy after my dismissal from the CIA, and that I was obviously upset. And they could deduce that I was to have been a CIA deep-cover officer.

To the best of my knowledge, Yurchenko never said a thing about having met or recruited me. I think that the FBI and CIA believed that if they threw the "Robert" description in my face, I would incriminate myself. But I never batted an eyelash, because I wasn't guilty. I never communicated with the Soviets before I walked into their embassy in Helsinki in September, 1985, and no evidence exists to the contrary.

It doesn't make sense that the KGB would give up a small fish—me—to save a big fish—Ames. Burning an agent is never good policy, but if it has to be done, you wouldn't do it through a man like Yurchenko, who would spend three months in the CIA's control. They could have given him truth serum and polygraphs, and they might have offered him millions of dollars to become a double agent. The KGB insists on tight control of their officers, and it is unlikely that they would ever have let Yurchenko embark on such a mission. Safer ways exist to burn an agent, such as planned gaps in communication security.

I've been asked many times how I feel about Yurchenko for putting me in the soup. In fact, I rarely think about him, have never met him and feel nothing about him. But tidbits I have gleaned over the years from General Kryuchkov and Igor have led me to this theory of Yurchenko:

Was he kidnapped by the FBI? No. The FBI and CIA have each used kidnapping as a tool in the past, but it is extremely unlikely that they would do so on a superpower diplomat of Yurchenko's status. They might be tempted to use it on me if they caught me in some banana republic, but not on him.

At the time he was debriefed, Yurchenko did not blow the whistle on Aldrich Ames, the shining star of all Soviet moles. Why?

Yurchenko had to give his new allies something in return for his hoped-for new life with his lover. One bargaining chip was Ronald Pelton, a spent agent. Another was "Robert," the target agent who looked good in the KGB's eyes and fit the profile of a bad boy to the CIA. I believe Yurchenko was holding on to his trump card—Ames—as insurance, and for possible use later. A wise man samples the goods before he pays for them, and defecting spies commonly hold information in reserve to ensure that bargains are kept as promised. And for re-negotiation when their money runs out.

Yurchenko had left an unhappy marriage behind in Moscow. In the West, he hoped to resume a romantic liaison with the wife of a Soviet diplomat stationed in Ottawa. The CIA permitted him to meet with his love interest. He discovered she would not leave her husband to come live with him. He became despondent, and decided he'd made a big mistake by defecting.

Yurchenko defected for love and money. The CIA and FBI were obsessed with finding a super-mole who could account for the loss of so many secrets and assets. The Americans bagged Pelton, then turned up the heat on me with accusations and heavy surveillance. I ran for my own protection, giving the FBI a black eye and the Soviets an unexpected propaganda victory. Then Yurchenko re-defected, with the same result. Ames and other moles remained safely in place, passing along file after file of the CIA's top secrets, while the media made of meal of me.

Chapter Twenty-Eight

Issues, Answers and a Proposal

Over the last nine years, I've had plenty of time to think about my case. It revolves around two issues: probation violation and espionage. My flight from the United States is not an issue in itself, for at the time I escaped the FBI and flew to Copenhagen and Helsinki, I had not been charged with any crime, and hence, was not a fugitive from justice.

Accusation: Howard must be guilty of espionage because he ran from the FBI and sought political asylum in the Soviet Union.

Response: At the time I took flight, I felt I could not get a fair trial in the United States. I never intended to leave the United States permanently. I hoped that within a year my name would be cleared and the FBI and CIA would find the true source of the CIA losses in the Soviet Union. When the FBI interrogated me in Santa Fe in August of 1985, I told them, "You guys have a leak somewhere. You're trying to hang it on me, and I won't let you do it." The FBI and CIA didn't even start looking for a mole until 1991 and didn't arrest him until 1994, while I took the blame for the loss of every technical secret and human asset in Moscow.

At the time I left, I was on probation for my New Mexico assault charge. The FBI could have had me thrown into jail for probation violation at any time because of my unauthorized European trips.

Accusation: Howard admitted sitting across the street from the Soviet consulate one day, contemplating espionage.

Response: This is true. Contemplation is one thing; commission quite another. I knew the Soviet consulate was not under surveillance by the FBI from my CIA training. As an intellectual exercise, it was interesting to think about how I could make contact with the Soviets without being noticed. Is this kind of fantasizing unusual? No. How many of us have ever walked into a bank and wondered how we would rob the place?

Accusation: Howard had the motive and the opportunity to be a Soviet spy.

Response: I was certainly an angry man with an axe to grind when the CIA dismissed me in 1983. But during the next year and a half, I accepted my fate and adjusted to a new life and job in New Mexico. I still regarded the Soviet Union as the "evil empire," and I would never have risked my family's welfare, my job and comfortable, suburban lifestyle to spy for them.

As to opportunity, I had been trained as a spy to work in Moscow, and I possessed secrets. But the combination of motivation and opportunity does not make a spy. That takes action, and I took none. I had no contact with the Soviets before contacting them in Helsinki, and I fully deserve the presumption of innocence.

Accusation: Howard took three suspicious trips to Europe at a time when he was accused of collaborating with the Soviets.

Response: I have always enjoyed European travel and I wanted a European assignment when I was with the CIA. My first trip was for legislative business and pleasure, the second was for pleasure and the third was to sell my Peruvian *huacos.*

Accusation: Howard had $10,000 hidden in the desert. The money must have come from the KGB.

Response: That I had stashed $10,000 in cash and coins in the desert was certainly eccentric, but that's all. I wanted to hide the proceeds from the sale of the Peruvian *huacos*— about $4,500— from the IRS The rest came from my own savings. I wasn't rich, but Mary and I were both working. The total was not a great deal of money for someone of my age and salary.

Question: Did the FBI ever find secret information in my possession in 1985?

Response: No, not a shred. I was clean as a whistle, even after a thorough search of my house and office.

Question: During the past nine years, has Howard ever confessed to the espionage charges brought against him in Santa Fe?

Response: No. Never in my meetings with the FBI in Santa Fe or in Stockholm did I ever confess to conveying any U.S. national defense information to a foreign power. Here in Moscow, where I am safe, I have also never made such a confession. Even if I had total recall and told the Soviets every scrap of information I knew in 1985, the value of any national defense material I had would have been no more damaging than that published openly in Daniel Ellsberg's book, *Papers on the War (The Pentagon Papers)* or Philip Agee's book, *Inside the Company,* the authors of which are free men today.

So Why Not Return?

Some of my critics have said, "If Howard is so innocent, why doesn't he go back and fight the espionage charges in court?" It's a legitimate question. My answer is complex. I have no doubt, I could not be proven guilty in court of espionage. However, I am vulnerable to prosecution on several other grounds, the combination of which makes it imprudent for me to return.

The first is the violation of my probation agreement with Santa Fe County on the assault conviction. Two of my three trips to Europe appear to violate that agreement, as does my flight to evade the FBI in September of 1985. Conviction on probation violation would probably get me about five years in jail.

Second, I haven't filed U.S. income taxes for nine years. The KGB wouldn't let me visit the U.S. embassy and file for several years, but I don't think the IRS would accept that as a valid excuse. Conviction on those charges might get me five years.

Third, I used a false passport to visit the United States in 1986. That could get me about two years. I never studied law, but there's nothing wrong with my arithmetic skills. The sentences listed above add up to at least twelve years imprisonment. I would probably beat the espionage charge, so they would throw the book at me on the other charges and make me serve the terms consecutively rather than concurrently. I am forty-two years old as I write this, and if I were to beat the espionage charge and was convicted of the others, I'd be in prison until I am in my mid-fifties. No thanks.

Even if I were to return and be acquitted on every charge, what kind of life could I make in the United States today? How would I make a living? Who would hire an ex-CIA spy accused of espionage? There is another issue, one of personal security, with which I would have to contend. There are some gung-ho, ex-military people in the CIA who would not be above against inflicting their own form of justice upon me no matter what a jury decided. These people, like those in the CIA's Special Operations Group, could easily arrange my accidental death. To the reader this may seem like a far-fetched, paranoid notion, but I rubbed shoulders with some of these guys and I know they'd be delighted to have the chance to terminate me for my giving their enemy a propaganda victory.

Here in Moscow, I have my own business. I have friends, my *dacha*, my apartment and regular visits from my wife and son. I lead a quiet, interesting and productive life. Can the U.S. force Russia to hand me over as part of some future aid pact? I don't think so. Both the U.S. and Russia harbor defectors.

The CIA's handling of the Howard, Yurchenko and Ames cases makes it clear that the Agency continues to make wholesale blunders in its basic attitudes and operations. Again and again, the Agency refuses to clean up its own act and reform practices for which any manager in private business would be fired. In my case, the CIA decided to terminate me immediately when they found problems with my polygraph tests. They never discussed any issues with me. They never considered moving me to a less-sensitive position for a probation period. They canned me on the spot, with no options for me, nothing.

There was the accusation that because I had previously used drugs, I should never have been hired. That contention is plainly ridiculous. In my generation, large numbers of college-educated men and women in America had experimented with drugs at some time in their lives, including President Bill Clinton and Newt Gingrich. The CIA had to hire ex-drug users in the 1980s, because probably half of their applicants were ex-drug users, and they knew it.

The CIA's fixation on the usefulness of the polygraph stands out like a sore thumb. I was fired because the polygraph indicated that I was hiding some kind of criminal activity, which I wasn't. Aldrich Ames breezed right through two similar polygraph tests while he was serving as the Soviet Union's hardest-working spy inside the CIA.

There is some hope for change. In March of 1994, CIA Director R. James Woolsey was quoted as saying that "he believed the polygraph had limited uses," and " considered it an essentially medieval instrument that could not serve as the basis of a modern security system." As Congressman Dan Glickman noted, "The history of the intelligence community shows it does not reward leaders who want to break with the traditions of the past."

Now the FBI. They have little to crow about in the handling of my case. When they decide to confront somebody about an alleged crime as serious as espionage, they should have some evidence to support their charges. When they came to confront me, all they had was an empty briefcase and a dream list.

In my case, the FBI thought they had a bad apple, but that's all. They thought through heavy-handed interrogation they would break me down and I'd give them the evidence they didn't possess. This just doesn't happen with two types of suspects: innocent people and people professionally-trained to withstand intelligence interrogations. I was both. The fact that one rusty ex-CIA agent could escape so easily from around-the-clock surveillance by sixty FBI agents never ceases to amaze me.

A Proposal

If I were the U.S. government attorney responsible for my case, I would show some degree of flexibility in the interest of closing my case. Why not say, "Okay, Howard, you come back and face only the original espionage charge we confronted you with in Santa Fe, and we will not pursue the related charges (flight, probation violations, tax issues, etc.)—just what caused this whole mess: espionage. You beat that original 1985 charge and you're home free."

That would be an offer I would find hard to refuse. Such an offer would be in the interest of the public, which seeks an answer to this affair. But it probably won't be made. Why not? Two reasons: One, their case against me was already tough to prove in 1985. Now, after Ames, it would be impossible. Two, the FBI and CIA have had their noses rubbed in the dirt over me for many years and they would prefer for me to live in Moscow rather than walk free in the U.S.A., where I would be a constant reminder of their institutional deficiencies.

Chapter Twenty-Nine

Ed Howard's Moscow

My state-owned *dacha* at Zhukovka is as comfortable as an old shoe. When I first arrived, the village was a restricted area, off-limits to foreigners and home to many senior politicians and KGB officials. Leonid Brezhnev's grandson lives here, along with a famous artist and the families of fifteen scientists who developed the Soviet atom bomb.

New *dachas* are popping up like mushrooms, and the area is suffering urban sprawl. With the Russian government facing a severe money crunch, I may not be able to keep my *dacha* forever. But if I have to move, I'll try to stay in Zhukovka.

When I drive to my office in Moscow, I go through Razdori, where the official country *dacha* of Russian President Boris Yeltsin is situated. Sometimes he takes his helicopter to work, but more often than not, he travels by car. If I leave Zhukovka exactly at 8:25 a.m., I reach Razdori at 8:35, about five minutes ahead of his limousine. The *militzia* blocks the side roads ahead of him, which makes it much easier for me, traveling on the main highway. His limousine, traveling at fairly high speed, will usually pass me about where we reach *Kuttovsky Prospekt*. Of course, I have to pull over and stop when his four-car entourage cruises by, but as soon as he passes me, I maneuver right behind him and hit the accelerator all the way into the center of Moscow. Yeltsin saves me ten minutes of traffic most mornings.

I have renovated my downtown apartment with European appliances. I use it occasionally when I have late business in the city.

I read books, especially action books. Robert Ludlum and John LeCarre are among my favorites. Ronald Kessler, author of *Moscow Station* upset everyone here because he focused on the wives of diplomats having sex parties with U.S. Marine Guards.

I keep in touch with the world through the *Wall Street Journal* and the *International Herald Tribune*.

Once a month I attend the ballet, usually the Bolshoi. My favorite is *Don Quixote*—or anything with a Spanish or Latin flavor. I visit the Pushkin Museum and other art galleries two or three times a year for special shows. My real pleasure is taking friends out to dinner at the *Tren-Mos Bistro* (an American-Russian joint venture), the Radisson or Pizza Hut.

There is a seedier side to Moscow, but since the 1980s I have avoided it. When I first arrived, I was wild and crazy. Now I have a stable life, and much of that stability stems from my work. Even though I'm the boss, I can't afford to walk in at ten in the morning with a hangover.

Someone asked me if Moscow has a "spook bar," where all the defectors, spies and intelligence agents hang out and play poker. Sorry, there is no such place. Moscow has two groups of expatriates. One, foreign businessmen who represent major companies such as Texaco, IBM and Proctor & Gamble. They hang out at expensive, foreign restaurants like *Aerostar* and the *Theatro Metro*. The other group, young entrepreneurs and Yuppie-wannabes who don't have much money. They are the sweater-and-blue jeans crowd who belly up to the Irish Bar on *Novy Arbat*.

My mother and father try to visit me at least once a year. My sister, Debra, and her son have made the trip three times in eight years. I speak with my parents and with Mary and

Lee at least once a week, and we all exchange letters by fax. My mailed letters reach them, but I rarely receive anything they send. No big conspiracy against me—just the inefficient Russian postal system.

I am almost wholly independent of the KGB, by mutual preference. In 1994 my KGB guards were mostly absent. I asked my KGB friends about this and was told, " When we have some new recruits, we use you as someone for them to practice surveillance on for a few days."

When I travel outside Russia, I take common-sense precautions. I don't advertise my travel in advance, and I am careful with whom I associate. I'm no longer worried about the FBI or CIA kidnapping me in Moscow, but I am concerned when I travel to Switzerland and Austria.

When Lieutenant General Mikhail Kolesnikov, chief of the Russian Armed Forces General Staff announced publicly that Aldrich Ames worked for Moscow, I thought that he should have been investigated for security violations. It's not the job of an intelligence officer, whether CIA or KGB, to publicly identify an agent of theirs, spent or not. You destroy the credibility of your intelligence service by doing so.

When I returned from Sweden, the KGB announced that I had been "a friend of Soviet intelligence for a number of years." I picked up the telephone and raised hell. The KGB denied having made the statement, but two Western news organizations had already picked it up. Yes, I had been a "friend," to the KGB, but to some people, a "friends of Soviet intelligence" is a man who gives them hard information and gets agents shot in Moscow—and I hadn't.

My current friends fall into two groups: those in the intelligence community and those I've met in my village and through business. For obvious reasons, I tend to avoid Americans.

I have a close relationship with my translator who speaks fluent English and lives in the same town as I do. Whenever I want to speak English, I turn to her.

Over the years, George Blake and I have developed a close personal relationship.

I still have contact with Igor and Sasha, my KGB companions from the early days.

I am also friendly with a number of young Swedish businessmen. Having barbecues with two or three close friends at my *dacha* is what I enjoy the most.

I exercise at a health club in one of the major American hotels two or three times a week, the same club where President Clinton worked out when he visited Moscow—we used the same treadmill and sweated in the same sauna! I use weights for general body toning and to keep my arms strong, and sit-ups to keep my abdomen flat. I love the sauna afterwards.

I enjoy tennis, and I often play with Sasha at the KGB sports complex, *Dinamo*. I also enjoy fishing in the Moscow River, ten minutes from my *dacha*.

My other good friend is Dr. Boris Ivanovitch, a physician who gave me hypnosis a number of years ago. Boris is both my landlord and a shareholder in my consulting business.

I'm the director of my own small legally-incorporated Russian company. My office is located near Moscow's International Trade Center, where I employ a translator and a financial analyst, and have sixteen Russian business consultants on tap. We deal with foreign and Russian clients who have start-up, accounting, marketing or legal problems.

Eighty percent of my business is deal-structuring for foreign businessmen, then looking after their interests when they're not in town.

I lost money the first year, broke even the second, and in 1994, my third year, I expect to make a small profit. Most of the rules I learned in business school don't apply in Russia— the economy is too primitive and explosive. My assets are my patience, guts and a sense of humor.

The Russian government's Statistical Committee estimated recently that ninety percent of all businesses in Russia do not turn a profit, and of those who do, only four in ten earn an honest profit! The hostile business climate here is aggravated by the mafia, unfriendly banks and a mammothly inefficient government bureaucracy.

Russian banks are notorious for user-unfriendliness. Dozens of forms and stamps are required to open an account. My bank, The Russian National Commercial Bank, once told me that they didn't like my signature on a document and asked me to re-sign it. I did so in front of the teller, asking for her advice on how to do it to her standards!

Next a businessman encounters the Russian Tax Inspectorate. They have enough ambiguous rules and regulations to make the IRS seem logical. If, for example, you take a client to lunch and expect to deduct it as a business expense, you must have him sign a document to that effect. Then you are entitled to take the lunch expenses from your profits— but not count it as a cost of doing business!

A Russian news organization recently reported that as many as eighty percent of businesses pay protection fees to the mafia. They visited my office, offering "protection" for a fee. I turned them down because we have our own security guards.

Bribery—say, for an import license—is so much a part of life that businessmen rarely complain about it any more. Bribery and extortion are part of the normal cost of staying in business.

One day a drunken fire chief came calling at our building, announcing that he had wrecked his Volvo the day before. He told my landlord that he would close our offices as a fire hazard unless we either immediately installed a sprinkler system—or paid him enough to fix his Volvo. We fixed his Volvo, the less expensive option.

In March 1993, my Russian night watchman proudly told me that I had received a fax from an "American client" during the night. The fax cover sheet read " U.S. Federal Bureau of Investigation." It was from Special Agent John Hudenko in Albuquerque. He proposed that he and the U.S. District Attorney come to Moscow and meet me at the U.S. embassy in early May 1993.

I read the short fax with interest. Did they want to make a deal?

I showed the fax to my old KGB contact and was advised not to answer it. Curiosity got the better of me. I sent the FBI a fax, asking them to state their agenda. I wrote that I would not meet at the embassy, which is U.S. territory, but proposed a meeting at the International Trade Center. Agent Hudenko responded three days later. He wrote that the FBI was not prepared to give me an outline of their agenda.

It seemed obvious that they simply wanted to repeat what they'd said in Stockholm: "Come home voluntarily and we'll go easier on you." I have the same answer now as then: No thanks.

There are many things I miss about the United States. I miss relatives; I miss the high desert and pine trees of New Mexico; Skippy peanut butter and Kool-Aid. I'll take another covert trip to the U.S.A. one day, as a tourist.

In ten years, I hope to have built up my consulting business to the point where I can work half-time as its chief consultant—come in, check the mail, talk with the manager, give my advice, and otherwise lead a relatively secluded life.

In New Mexico, I would probably have been a cattle rancher. Here, I'd like to go out to Lake Baikal, live in a wooden cabin with a dog, a Jeep and a fishing rod—plus a computer and modem. That would be the cat's pajamas.

I no longer have to have my wife and son in the next room all the time to be happy. I can make do with twice-yearly visits, and the peace of mind that they are well looked after.

I want my American readers to know that I never intended to hurt my country, and that nothing I have done ever threatened the security of the United States or their families and children. I was never responsible for the arrest or death of anyone. The CIA, FBI and I all made mistakes, but on that fateful day in September, 1985, I thought I had no chance except flight. I don't expect forgiveness, but I hope for understanding.

The past nine years of my life have been extraordinary. Ten years ago, I never thought I would visit the Soviet Union. Five years ago, I never thought I would see the disintegration and collapse of the Soviet Union.

In grade school we read Edward Everett Hale's book, *The Man Without A Country*. At the time I thought how sad it was—and how absurd. How could anyone not have a country?

In 1986, when I was in the Soviet Union secretly, I remembered that book, and the memory depressed me. It was a true story—and I was the main character. My depression continued until I learned two simple principles.

First, take life one day at a time and make the most of it. Then, as now, it was important for me to maintain a positive mental attitude.

Second, be comfortable with whatever you have at the end of the day.

That combination—a positive mental attitude and a realistic outlook on what it was possible for me to accomplish kept me from committing suicide, as many others in my situation had done before me.

At various times in our lives we must pause and take stock of our lives, learn our lessons, say goodbye to the past and move on. The writing of this book completes in large part my effort to come to grips with the circumstances, events and decisions that took me from Santa Fe to Moscow.

I started writing this book in Budapest in 1988 as a memoir for my son. Its title then was *The Enemy of My Enemy* and it was designed to be a damning indictment of the CIA.

Today, I realize that this kind of anger only hurts the one who holds it. Latin people have a proverb about this: "The man bent on revenge should dig two graves: one for his enemy and the other for himself."

In 1993 and 1994 I rewrote the book and changed the title to *Safe House*. I plan to spend the rest of my life in my safe house, looking toward the future, leaving the past behind me.

Appendix

Central Intelligence Agency
Publications Review Board
1016 Ames Building
Washington, D.C. 20505
Telephone No. (703) 351-2546

17 August 1994

Mr. Joel D. Joseph,
Attorney at Law
National Press Books
7200 Wisconsin Ave.
Bethesda, Maryland 20814

Dear Mr. Joseph:

The Publications Review Board has reviewed the manuscript of Mr. Edward Lee Howard's book, tentatively titled *Safe House*, which you submitted to the Board on his behalf, as his attorney. The Board has determined that the manuscript contains classified information and therefore requests that you advise Mr. Howard that he is not authorized to proceed with publication.

Due to the highly unusual, indeed unique, circumstances associated with this submission, the Board must decline to identify the classified passages in the manuscript. Mr. Howard's ongoing association with a foreign intelligence service makes it inappropriate for this Agency to affirm or authenticate to him those specific portions of his writings on intelligence related matters that are sensitive.

Further, because of Mr. Howard's fugitive status, we are obligated to inform the Department of Justice of Mr. Howard's manuscript and to provide to them the manuscript as well as our determinations about the classified nature of certain passages. We cannot comment further on Mr. Howard's manuscript, pending resolution of his status with the Department of Justice.

   Please direct any comments or questions on this entire
matter to Ms. Kathleen McGinn, Office of General Counsel,
Central Intelligence Agency, Washington, DC 20505.

   Thank you for your and your client's cooperation in the
review process; enclosed for your and your client's
information is a copy of the pertinent Headquarters
Regulation 6-2.

Sincerely,

Molly J. Tasker
Chair, Publications Review Board

CENTRAL INTELLIGENCE AGENCY

WASHINGTON, D.C. 20505

Office of General Counsel

23 August 1994

Joel D. Joseph,
Counsel
National Press Books
7200 Wisconsin Avenue
Bethesda, Maryland 20814

Dear Mr. Joseph:

As I informed you during our meeting yesterday, Edward
Lee Howard's manuscript contains the names of Central
Intelligence Agency covert employees. Because the
manuscript contains such information as well as other
classified information, Mr. Howard is not authorized to
proceed with publication. In addition, please be advised
that publication of this manuscript may constitute a
violation of the Intelligence Identities Protection Act of
1982, 50 U.S.C. Section 421 et seq., and any publication of
this manuscript in its current form may result in
prosecution of Mr. Howard and of other parties participating
in such publication, including the publishers.

If you have any questions or would care to discuss this
matter further, please telephone me at (703) 874-3121.

Very truly yours,

Kathleen A. McGinn
Assistant General Counsel

7200 Wisconsin Avenue
Bethesda, Maryland 20814
August 26, 1994   (301) 657-1616 (Fax) 657-8475

Leo Hazelwood
Executive Director
Central Intelligence Agency
Washington, DC 20505

Dear Mr. Hazelwood,

This letter is an appeal of the decision of the
Publications Review Board dated August 17, 1994 concerning
prepublication review of a book by Edward Lee Howard,
tentatively titled <u>Safe House</u>.   The undersigned represents
Mr. Howard in this appeal.

This book is substantially an autobiography of Edward
Lee Howard. It pleads his case that he did nothing illegal
and did not harm the security interests of the United
States. This publication is an exercise of Mr. Howard's
first amendment rights of free speech and of the right to
petition the government for redress of grievances. Mr.
Howard also wants to present his book to appropriate members
of the Congress of the United States.

Now I understand that some of the material in his book
will be embarrassing to the Agency. I also understand that
the material is critical of the Agency. After all Mr.
Howard did manage to avoid arrest in the United States on
several occasions. However, the prepublication review
regulations specifically provide:

   h (2) Permission to publish will not be denied solely
   because the statement may be embarrassing to or
   critical of the Agency.

The Publication Review Board refused to suggest
deletion or revision of parts of this book.   The letter
from the review board gives no guidance as to what should be
deleted.   The prepublication review regulations provide
that the Agency's policy is to "identify information for
deletion or revision only to the extent necessary to protect
information the disclosure of which would harm national
security." HR 6-2, a(4)(a).

The agency and the Publication Review Board have failed
to comply with this policy and utterly fail to give Mr.
Howard any guidance.

AMERICA'S MOST TALKED ABOUT BOOKS

Earlier this week I met with Kathleen McGinn at the general counsel's office. She provided me with more specific information as to what was objectionable to the agency. She stated that the names of agents were disclosed. Mr. Howard will change the names in question, except the names of the author and Aldrich Ames, to pseudonyms to avoid compromising the individuals in question.

Neither Mr. Howard nor I have any desire to compromise the national security interests of the United States. However, Mr. Howard has a first amendment right to publish his book, and the American people and the Congress have the right to read his book, which presents his side of this unfortunate case. Please expedite this matter and provide me with the additional information that you want deleted or revised in Mr. Howard's manuscript before publication. I am willing to meet with you or the Director to work this matter out. I do not believe that protracted litigation is in the best interests of the United States, the American public or Edward Lee Howard.

Sincerely yours,

Joel D. Joseph

Central Intelligence Agency

Washington, D.C. 20505

27 October 1994

Joel D. Joseph
Attorney at Law
National Press Books
7200 Wisconsin Avenue
Bethesda, Maryland 20814

Dear Mr. Joseph:

Senior Agency officials have completed a comprehensive review of the Publications Review Board's decision concerning the manuscript you submitted on behalf of Edward Lee Howard. Based upon the results of this review, I affirm the Publications Review Board's determination that the manuscript contains classified information and, consequently, that Mr. Howard is not authorized to proceed with publication. I also affirm the Publications Review Board's determination that the Agency will not identify the specific classified passages contained in the manuscript. In that regard, the Board's decision was based upon Mr. Howard's legal status as a fugitive and his ongoing association with a foreign intelligence service. Each of these two factors independently provides sufficient justification for the Agency's refusal to identify classified information.

Sincerely,

Leo Hazlewood
Executive Director

Index